*was only sent to complete the virtuous content of character.*

PROPHET MUḤAMMAD ﷺ

THE CONTENT *of* CHARA

# The Content *of* Character

## ETHICAL SAYINGS OF THE PROPHET MUḤAMMAD

صلى الله عليه وسلم

*Translation and Introduction by*
Hamza Yusuf

*Collected by*
Shaykh Al-Amin Ali Mazrui

*Foreword by*
Ali Mazrui

SANDALA

Published by Sandala, Inc., 2015
www.sandala.org
info@sandala.org


Revised Edition.



ISBN-10: 0985565934

ISBN-13: 978-0-9855659-3-0

Printed in the United States of America

Project Director: Hamza Yusuf
Project Manager: Aisha Subhani
Cover Design and Layout: Ian Abdallateef Whiteman

Special note of gratitude for the following people who assisted in the completion of the this text:

Tom Devine, Uzma Husaiini, Tahira Larmore, Ismael Nass, Erik Yusuf Habecker, Mazin Halabi, Imam Zaid Shakir, Shaykh Jamal Zahabi, Dr. Fawzia Bariun, Dr. Asad Tarsin, Mariam Jukaku, Sadia Shakir, and a special thanks to Aaron Spevack for his work on the biographies.

# CONTENTS

Foreword
vii

Introduction
xi

Sayings of the Prophet ﷺ
1

Translator's Note
41

Biographies of the Narrators
49

# Foreword

Shaykh Al-Amīn bin ʿAlī Mazrūʿī was my father. He was born in January of 1891 (1308 AH) in Mombasa, Kenya. He came from a family of distinguished Islamic scholars. His own father, Shaykh ʿAlī bin ʿAbdallāh Mazrūʿī, was a graduate of Islamic institutions in Mecca in the 19th century.

Shaykh Al-Amīn was exposed to some of the reformist Islamic ideas coming out of Egypt. He was influenced by the new waves of thought of such thinkers as Muḥammad ʿAbduh, Rashīd Riḍa, and Jamāl ad-Dīn al-Afghānī. Al-Amīn had also studied among distinguished Islamic scholars in Zanzibar (now part of Tanzania) and Lamu, along the Coast of Kenya. Educationally, Al-Amīn was especially indebted to the Cadi (Judge) of Mombasa at the time, Shaykh Sulaymān ʿAlī Mazrūʿī, whose eldest daughter, Swafiya, Al-Amīn subsequently married. Swafiya was my mother.

I was born about the time when Shaykh Al-Amīn was appointed Cadi of Mombasa in succession to Shaykh Sulaymān in the early 1930's. In 1937 (1355 AH), Al-Amīn became the Chief Cadi of the whole of Kenya. He remained Chief Cadi for almost ten years, and he died in April 1947.

What is the significance of Shaykh Al-Amīn ʿAlī Mazrūʿī for Islam in East Africa? Among the Islamic scholars of Eastern Africa, he probably ranked among the top five in quality of scholarship and literary influence through his books. He wrote in both Kiswahili (Swahili) and the Arabic language. Paradoxically, his best known work in the West is a work of dynastic history. It was translated by Reverend James McL. Ritchie and published by Oxford University Press on behalf of the British Academy. Oxford published the book under the title of *The History of the Mazru'i Dynasty of Mombasa* (1995) and included the original Arabic text in the same volume.

Shaykh Al-Amīn ʿAlī Mazrūʿī symbolized an intellectual bridge linking diverse traditions. Among Islamic scholars in sub-Saharan Africa, he symbolized a bridge between orthodox Islam and the more modernist tendencies symbolized by Muḥammad ʿAbduh and Jamāl ad-Dīn al-Afghānī. Al-Amīn was also a bridge between Islamic scholarship in the Arabic language and Islamic scholarship in African tongues.

The majority of his publications were in the Swahili language, but he constantly championed the importance of the Arabic language at all levels of Islamic education. He hired a native Arabic speaker to tutor me in the Arabic language, as he tried to live by his own principles in the education of his own children.

Shaykh Al-Amīn also attempted to be a bridge between the media and the academy as a tool of Islamic education. He founded a newspaper called *Al-Iṣlāḥ* in 1932, which was published in both Kiswahili and Arabic. He also inaugurated another newspaper more exclusively in Kiswahili in 1930 called *Aṣ-Ṣaḥīfa*. Shaykh Al-Amīn did not have the resources to sustain these publications for very long, but they did signify the phase of "academia"—the academy and the media—in Shaykh Al-Amīn's bridge-building career.

As a scholar, Shaykh Al-Amīn also attempted to be a bridge between Islam and modernity. He argued that while Christianity became the vanguard of progress when it became more secular and less Christian, Islam was the vanguard of progress when it was more Islamic and less secular. According to Al-Amīn, progress among Muslims required not the abandonment of Islam but the recovery of the original spirit of Islamic enlightenment.

Shaykh Al-Amīn's choice of these favored sayings of the Prophet ﷺ was influenced by his effort to be a bridge-builder, especially between the values of tradition and the norms of modernity, between the wisdom of religion and the compassion of humanity.

ʿALĪ A. MAZRŪʿĪ
(1425 AH/2005 CE)

*Professor ʿAlī Mazrūʿī (d. 1435* AH/2014 CE*) was a world-renowned scholar, educator and prolific writer in the field of African studies and intellectual political culture. He was born into a Muslim household rich with scholars including his own father who was the Chief Qadi (Islamic judge) of Kenya. He grew up immersed in Swahili culture, Islamic traditional sciences, and Western education achieving fluency in Swahili, Arabic, and English. After completing his doctorate from Oxford University, Professor Mazrūʿī joined Makerere University in Uganda where he served as the head of the Department of Political Science and Dean of the Faculty of Social Sciences. In 1974, he joined the faculty of the University of Michigan and fifteen years later was appointed to the faculty of Binghamton University, State University of New York, as the Albert Schweitzer Professor in the Humanities and the Director of the Institute of Global Cultural Studies (IGCS). A true intellectual giant, Professor Mazrūʿī authored over forty books and numerous articles and essays. He also wrote and narrated the famous television series, "The Africans: A Triple Heritage". The influence of his scholarly teachings and writings will resonate for years to come.*

# Introduction

## By Hamza Yusuf

### LISTENING TO THE PROPHET

Can we change by listening? Can we be so touched and inspired by words that we are moved to renew and remake ourselves as better, nobler, and more merciful human beings? The impact that good words have had on humanity throughout history resoundingly declares we can.

These wise sayings of the Prophet Muḥammad ﷺ, collected here, are designed to do just that—to guide us to the very best in ourselves. Compiled by the renowned East African scholar, Al-Amīn ʿAlī Mazrūʿī, this collection brings together sayings that encourage good character. By listening closely, we may hear something that speaks to us, speaks to our conscience and our heart, and moves us to become better human beings.

For Muslims, Muḥammad is a messenger from God. He occupies a central position in Islam, both as the vessel for God's speech and as the primary interpreter of the Qur'an's meanings. In Islam, hadiths, or sayings of the Prophet ﷺ are second only to the Qur'an as a source for legal, ethical, and spiritual guidance. In essence, they are a commentary on the word of God as expressed in the Qur'an.

Listening is the key. Many of us in the West have never listened to the Prophet Muḥammad ﷺ himself. We may have heard many things said about him, but we have not actually listened to his own words. These sayings offer us the opportunity to do just that. They allow us to enter into an internal dialogue with his words, and, through them to begin to know a man whom Muslims, and even some Western historians, believe to be the most significant human being who ever lived. They also offer us an opportunity to be introduced personally to someone whom many of our human family revere as a fount of mercy, compassion, wisdom, justice, and love. All we have to do is listen.

The Prophet's ﷺ words are as vital and relevant today as they were fourteen hundred years ago when they were first spoken. Whether you are a Muslim, a practitioner of another faith, or even someone who has no religious belief, these sayings have much to teach us. Sayings such as "A kind word is charity" and "Love for humanity what you love for yourself," speak to us regardless of our personal creed; they speak to our shared essential nature.

They are also a way to understand better a large segment of our fellow human beings. By learning what Muslims around the world really believe, we edify ourselves regarding people about whom we may hold prejudicial and erroneous opinions.

Perhaps even more importantly for us as individuals, the hadiths are also a way to know our own selves better. They function as mirrors—by looking into them, we may come to see ourselves more clearly. We may come to see our humanity, the best and worst of ourselves. And through this seeing, this reflection, we may be moved to change ourselves to be more conformed to principled behavior. These sayings reflect back to us something that is within ourselves. If we see something noble that touches our hearts, we are seeing the best in ourselves. And if we see something we resist, it is perhaps something within ourselves that we resist. In a sense, we could say that these sayings read us as we are reading them. Each saying is an opportunity to know our selves more intimately.

Each saying is also a way to know more intimately the man who first uttered them. They can provide an opening into the one who, for Muslims, is the embodiment of impeccable character; the Prophet ﷺ says, "I was only sent to perfect noble character." These sayings are more than just his words; they are the verbal expressions of his personal conduct. As one of his companions, ʿAmr bin Al-ʿĀṣ said, "We saw everything the Prophet taught us embodied in his own character." The Prophet's teachings offer us a glimpse of what propelled his companions to love and cherish him to such a degree.

Another benefit of studying the Prophet's ﷺ words is that we can sense to some degree the power of words that impelled the Arabs to burst forth upon the theater of history with a vigor that restored vitality to countless peoples. Imām al-Būṣayrī says in his *Poem of the Cloak*:

> Finally his light dawned on the horizon,
> And his radiant guidance suffused the world and brought life to
> Countless civilizations.

For Muslims, the reason the Prophet's ﷺ words resonated so profoundly in the hearts of Arabs, and drove them from their homes with a passionate desire to convey them to others, is their celestial source.

Humanity's desire to receive guidance from heaven is universal. Whether it be the Confucian "Heavenly Mandate," the Delphic Oracle's adage "As above, so below," or Emerson's "Hitch your wagon to a star," we seek celestial lights to guide us. The New Testament says that Christ, ﷺ prayed, "Thy will be done, on earth as it is in heaven." In this simple yet profound petition is that universal desire to connect with the heavens, to embody celestial character: to coordinate personal will with Divine will, to align the earthly with heavenly order. For in doing so, we achieve the pinnacle and full realization of our humanity. It is, in essence, Islam: submission to the will of the Divine.

According to Islam, submitting to the will of God is achieved through following the example of the prophets. The

Qur'an says, "You have in Abraham an excellent example." Each age had its prophet and its practice; for the Muslims, the Prophet Muḥammad ﷺ is the paragon for humanity's last universal phase. Following the Prophet ﷺ means following his kindness to animals, his gentleness with children, his concern for the weak and oppressed, his care of the orphan and the widow, and his deep practice of justice always tempered with mercy. It means modeling oneself on his character.

The desire to model oneself on another emanates from love. There are four primary types of love, each corresponding to the respective experiences in the lover's heart. The first is the initial attraction to the beloved's sheer physical beauty. The second results from a recognition of the good received at the beloved's hand. The third arises from a gnosis of the beloved's internal beauty and merits. And finally, the fourth is the love that is solely for the sake of God, known in the West as *caritas*. Desirous of instilling profound love in the hearts of believers, the early Muslims left behind precise descriptions of the Prophet's ﷺ physical appearance, his actions, his character, and his rank with God. One contemporary describes him in the following words:

> His face was luminous as the full moon. He was taller than average but not excessive in height. He had wavy hair, which he parted and which did not go beyond his shoulders, and he had fair skin and a wide brow. His eyes were black, his beard full, and his nose fine and aquiline. His cheeks were firm, and his teeth were brilliantly white with a small gap between the front ones. His physique was supple and lithe with a full chest and broad shoulders. His legs were powerful, his fingers slender, and his muscles fine and sinewy.
>
> When he spoke, he was always brief and reflective. He spoke when he saw benefit and spent long periods in silent contemplation. His speech was comprehensive, being neither wordy nor laconic. He had a mild temperament and was never harsh nor cruel, coarse nor rude. He expressed gratitude for everything given to him, no matter how

> insignificant. When he spoke, his companions lowered their heads as if birds were perched upon them. When he was silent, they felt free to speak. He never criticized food nor praised it excessively. He never uttered obscenities nor did he find fault in people. He did not flatter people but praised them when appropriate.

While the Prophet ﷺ took matters most seriously and was a deeply contemplative man, he was also the most balanced person and was lighthearted and even humorous when appropriate. In a world wherein religion is often dampened with dourness, it is refreshing that the Prophet ﷺ was known for his wonderful sense of humor.

The Prophet ﷺ said, "I joke, but always truthfully." A man once requested from the Prophet the use of a camel. He replied, "I can loan you a camel's foal."

"What use to me is a camel's foal?" queried the man.

Laughing, the Prophet quipped, "Isn't every camel the foal of another?"

Once, a gruff desert Bedouin urinated in the Prophet's mosque, which greatly angered some of the companions; had not the Prophet ﷺ constrained them, they would have attacked the Bedouin. The Prophet ﷺ kindly told the man that mosques were sacred places that should be kept pure and clean. Due to the companions' harshness towards him and the Prophet's ﷺ gentleness, the man cried, "O God, forgive me and Muḥammad and no one else."

The Prophet ﷺ laughed and said, "You are limiting the vast mercy of God."

The Prophet Muḥammad ﷺ is a man of many facets. He was the founder of a religion that embraces a fifth of humanity. He inspired a yet-to-be-rivaled civilization with brilliant spirituality, tolerance, and longevity. While he is worth knowing for all of these reasons, the real and most important reason is simply that he is a true and enlightened teacher who has much to teach us.

Although his historical and enduring meaning has always been worthy of interest, we have urgent need to listen to him today. Ignorance is greatly threatening the very real possibility of conciliation and conviviality among the diverse peoples of this planet, an ignorance that his teachings address directly. The Qur'an reminds us:

> *[God] created you from a male and a female, and made you a plurality of races and tribes for you to get to know each other. The most noble of you in the sight of God are those of you who are most conscientious. And God is omniscient, fully aware.*

Ironically, this dire need to listen to the Prophet Muḥammad ﷺ applies as much to some misguided Muslims as it does to peoples of other faiths and creeds. Perhaps if we in the West made greater efforts to remove the historical ignorance we have inherited by taking the Prophet ﷺ as seriously as he deserves to be taken, many people in the troubled East might reevaluate their own shortcomings in grasping his universal message of mercy and compassion. The 13th century Egyptian poet, Ibn al-Farīd, said:

> If the fragrance of his remembrance radiates in the West
> And a sick man resides in the East, he will recover.

Let us then all set out, in our own unique ways, to help remove the obstacles of ignorance from the path to peace. We can begin by seeing embedded in the word "ignorance" the word "ignore," and by recognizing that the world can no longer afford to ignore the Prophet Muḥammad ﷺ about whom the enlightened Victorian poet Edwin Arnold said:

> ...that marvelous and gifted Teacher created a vast empire of new belief and new civilization and prepared a sixth part of humanity for the developments and reconciliations which later times will bring. For Islam must be conciliated; it cannot be thrust scornfully aside or rooted out. It shares the task of the education of the world with its sister religions, and it will contribute its eventual portion to:

*"that far-off divine event,*
*Towards which the whole creation moves."*

The sayings collected here are ultimately meant as an introduction to that "marvelous and gifted Teacher" whom the Qur'an describes as "a mercy to all the worlds." Read each one slowly, contemplatively, letting it reveal its wisdom to you. As the Prophet ﷺ reminded us, "Consideration is from God, and haste is from Satan." Find one that speaks to you, and listen to it. Let it permeate you, and then in the example of the Prophet Muḥammad ﷺ try to implement it in your life. And return to them now and again as continual sources of guidance and wisdom.

ﷺ (*Ṣallallāhu ʿalayhī wa salam*)

This means "Peace and blessing of God be upon him" and is said by Muslims when the Prophet Muḥammad's name is heard or uttered, out of love and reverence for him.

ﷺ (*ʿAlayhis salām*)

This means "Peace be upon him" and is said by Muslims when any prophet's name is heard or uttered, out of love and reverence for them.

# The Ethical Sayings of the Prophet ﷺ

1. The Messenger of God ﷺ said, "Islam is clean, so cleanse yourselves, for only the cleansed shall enter Paradise." *Aṭ-Ṭabarānī*

2. The Messenger of God ﷺ said, "The characteristics of a hypocrite are three: when he speaks, he lies; when he gives his word, he breaks it; and when he is given a trust, he is unfaithful." *Al-Bukhārī and Muslim*

3. The Messenger of God ﷺ said, "Consideration is from God, and haste is from the devil." *Al-Bayhaqī*

4. The Messenger of God ﷺ said, "Keep God in mind wherever you are; follow a wrong with a right that offsets it; and treat people courteously." *At-Tirmidhī*

5. The Messenger of God ﷺ said, "Among those not graced with God's glance on the Day of Judgment are a severer of bonds of kin and an obnoxious neighbor." *Ad-Daylamī*

6. The Messenger of God ﷺ said, "Love for humanity what you love for yourself." *Ibn Mājah*

7. The Messenger of God ﷺ said, "Allow your food to cool a bit, for hot food lacks blessing." *Ad-Daylamī*

1 قَالَ رَسُولُ اللهِ صَلَّى اللهُ عَلَيهِ وَسَلَّمَ: «الإِسْلَامُ نَظِيفٌ فَتَنَظَّفُوا، فَإِنَّهُ لَا يَدْخُلُ الجَنَّةَ إِلَّا نَظِيفٌ» رَوَاهُ الطَّبَرَاني

2 قَالَ رَسُولُ اللهِ صَلَّى اللهُ عَلَيْهِ وَسَلَّمَ: «آيَةُ الـمُنَافِقِ ثَلَاثٌ: إِذَا حَدَّثَ كَذَبَ، وَإِذَا وَعَدَ أَخْلَفَ، وَإِذَا ائْتُمِنَ خَانَ»
رَوَاهُ البخاري ومسلم

3 قَالَ رَسُولُ اللهِ صَلَّى اللهُ عَلَيهِ وَسَلَّمَ: «التَّأَنِّي مِنَ اللهِ وَالعَجَلَةُ مِنَ الشَّيْطَانِ» رَوَاهُ البيهقي

4 قَالَ رَسُولُ اللهِ صَلَّى اللهُ عَلَيهِ وَسَلَّمَ: «اتَّقِ اللهَ حَيثُمَا كُنْتَ وَأَتْبِعِ السَّيِّئَةَ الحَسَنَةَ تَمْحُهَا، وَخَالِقِ النَّاسَ بِخُلُقٍ حَسَنٍ»
رَوَاهُ الترمذي

5 قَالَ رَسُولُ اللهِ صَلَّى اللهُ عَلَيهِ وَسَلَّمَ: «اِثْنَانِ لَا يَنْظُرُ اللهُ إِلَيْهِمَا يَوْمَ القِيَامَةِ: قَاطِعُ الرَّحِمِ وَجَارُ السُّوءِ» رَوَاهُ الديلمي

6 قَالَ رَسُولُ اللهِ صَلَّى اللهُ عَلَيهِ وَسَلَّمَ: «أَحِبَّ لِلنَّاسِ مَا تُحِبُّ لِنَفْسِكَ» رَوَاهُ ابن ماجه

7 قَالَ رَسُولُ اللهِ صَلَّى اللهُ عَلَيهِ وَسَلَّمَ: «أَبْرِدُوا بالطَّعَامِ، فَإِنَّ الحَارَّ لَا بَرَكَةَ فِيْهِ» رَوَاهُ الديلمي

8. The Messenger of God ﷺ said, "After obligatory rites, the action most beloved to God is delighting other Muslims." *Aṭ-Ṭabarānī*

9. The Messenger of God ﷺ said, "Should you become eager to mention another's faults, recall your own." *Ar-Rāfiʿī*

10. The Messenger of God ﷺ said, "Should you wish to act, ponder well the consequences. If good, carry on; if not, desist." *Ibn al-Mubārak*

11. The Messenger of God ﷺ said, "Should any of you burp or sneeze, let him stifle the sound." *Al-Bayhaqī*

12. The Messenger of God ﷺ said, "When a person dies, his deeds die with him, except for three: charitable endowments, beneficial knowledge, and righteous children who supplicate on his behalf." *Muslim*

13. The Messenger of God ﷺ said, "When any of you takes a meal, let him eat, drink, receive, and share with the right hand." *al-Qurṭubī*

8 قَالَ رَسُولُ اللهِ صَلَّى اللهُ عَلَيهِ وَسَلَّمَ: «أَحَبُّ الأَعْمَالِ إِلَىٰ اللهِ بَعْدَ الفَرَائِضِ إِدْخَالُ السُّرُورِ عَلَى المُسْلِمِ» رَوَاهُ الطبراني

9 قَالَ رَسُولُ اللهِ صَلَّى اللهُ عَلَيهِ وَسَلَّمَ: «إِذَا أَرَدْتَ أَنْ تَذْكُرَ عُيُوبَ غَيْرِكَ فَاذْكُرْ عُيُوبَ نَفْسِكَ» رَوَاهُ الرافعي

10 قَالَ رَسُولُ اللهِ صَلَّى اللهُ عَلَيهِ وَسَلَّمَ: «إِذَا أَرَدْتَ أَنْ تَفْعَلَ أَمْراً فَتَدَبَّرْ عَاقِبَتَهُ، فَإِنْ كَانَ خَيْراً فَامْضِهِ، وَإِنْ كَانَ شَرّاً فَانْتَهِ» رَوَاهُ ابن المبارك

11 قَالَ رَسُولُ اللهِ صَلَّى اللهُ عَلَيهِ وَسَلَّمَ: «إِذَا تَجَشَّأَ أَحَدُكُمْ أَوْ عَطَسَ فَلَا يَرفَعْ بِهِمَا الصَّوْتَ» رَوَاهُ البيهقي

12 قَالَ رَسُولُ اللهِ صَلَّى اللهُ عَلَيهِ وَسَلَّمَ: «إِذَا مَاتَ ابْنُ آدَمَ انْقَطَعَ عَمَلُهُ إِلَّا مِنْ ثَلَاثٍ: صَدَقَةٍ جَارِيَةٍ، أَو عِلْمٍ يُنْتَفَعُ بِهِ، أَو وَلَدٍ صَالِحٍ يَدعُو لَهُ» رَوَاهُ مسلم

13 قَالَ رَسُولُ اللهِ صَلَّى اللهُ عَلَيهِ وَسَلَّمَ: « إِذَا أَكَلَ أَحَدُكُم فَلْيَأْكُلْ بِيَمِينِهِ، وَلْيَشْرَبْ بِيَمِينِهِ، وَلْيَأْخُذْ بِيَمِينِهِ، وَلْيُعْطِ بِيَمِينِهِ» رَوَاهُ القرطبي

14. The Messenger of God ﷺ said, "Two should never converse privately excluding a third until others join them. The reason being is that it would dismay him." Al-Bukhārī *and Muslim*

15. The Messenger of God ﷺ said, "Should one of you yawn, let him place his hand over his mouth and avoid a yawner's howl. Even Satan derides the howling yawner." *Ibn Mājah*

16. The Messenger of God ﷺ said, "If your good deeds delight you and your foul deeds distress you, you are a believer." *Aḍ-Ḍiyyā'*

17. The Messenger of God ﷺ said, "If a people's dignitary pays a visit, honor him." *Ibn Mājah*

18. The Messenger of God ﷺ said, "Should one of you sneeze, say, 'Praise be to God, Lord of the worlds.' To that, his brother or companion should respond, 'May God have mercy on you.' If he says that, then the first should add, 'May God always guide you and keep aright your heart.'" Al-Bukhārī

19. The Messenger of God ﷺ said, "If one of you requests permission to enter a place and, after three requests, permission is yet not granted, he should leave." Al-Bukhārī *and Muslim*

14 قَالَ رَسُولُ اللهِ صَلَّى اللهُ عَلَيهِ وَسَلَّمَ: «إذا كُنْتُمْ ثَلاَثَةً فَلا يَتَنَاجَى اثنَانِ دُونَ الآخَرِ حَتَّى تَخْتَلِطُوا بِالنَّاسِ مِن أَجلِ أَنَّ ذَلِكَ يُحْزِنُهُ» رَوَاهُ البخاري ومسلم

15 قَالَ رَسُولُ اللهِ صَلَّى اللهُ عَلَيهِ وَسَلَّمَ: «إِذَا تَثَاءَبَ أَحَدُكُمْ فَلْيَضَعْ يَدَهُ عَلَى فِيهِ وَلَا يَعْوِي، فَإِنَّ الشَّيْطَانَ يَضْحَكُ مِنْهُ» رَوَاهُ ابن ماجه

16 قَالَ رَسُولُ اللهِ صَلَّى اللهُ عَلَيهِ وَسَلَّمَ: «إِذَا سَرَّتْكَ حَسَنَتُكَ وَسَاءَتْكَ سَيِّئَتُكَ فَأَنْتَ مُؤْمِنٌ» رَوَاهُ الضياء

17 قَالَ رَسُولُ اللهِ صَلَّى اللهُ عَلَيهِ وَسَلَّمَ: «إِذَا أَتَاكُمْ كَرِيمُ قَوْمٍ فَأَكْرِمُوهُ» رَوَاهُ ابن ماجه

18 قَالَ رَسُولُ اللهِ صَلَّى اللهُ عَلَيهِ وَسَلَّمَ: «إِذَا عَطَسَ أَحَدُكُمْ فَلْيَقُلِ الحَمْدُ لِلهِ رَبِّ العَالَمِينَ، وَلْيَقُلْ لَه أَخُوهُ أَوْ صَاحِبُهُ: يَرْحَمُكَ اللهُ، فَإذَا قَالَ لَهُ يَرْحَمُكَ اللهُ، فَليَقُلْ لَهُ: يَهْدِيْكُمُ اللهُ وَيُصْلِحُ بَالَكُمْ» رَوَاهُ البخاري

19 قَالَ رَسُولُ اللهِ صَلَّى اللهُ عَلَيهِ وَسَلَّمَ: «إِذَا اسْتَأْذَنَ أَحَدُكُمْ ثَلاثاً فَلَمْ يُؤْذَن لَهُ فَلْيَرْجِعْ» رَوَاهُ البخاري ومسلم

20. The Messenger of God ﷺ said, "If you happen to see a funeral procession, stand for it until it passes or the dead is laid to rest." *Al-Bukhārī and Muslim*

21 The Messenger of God ﷺ said, "Abandon desire for this world, and God will love you. Abandon desire for others' goods, and people will love you." *Ibn Mājah*

22. The Messenger of God ﷺ said, "Pursue knowledge even to China, for its pursuance is the sacred duty of every Muslim." *Ibn ʿAbdal-Barr*

23. The Messenger of God ﷺ said, "Since the successful are always envied, use discretion in fulfilling your needs." *Aṭ-Ṭabarānī*

24. The Messenger of God ﷺ said, "The most virtuous behavior is to engage those who sever relations, to give to those who withhold from you, and to forgive those who wrong you." *Imām Aḥmad*

25. The Messenger of God ﷺ said, "The best charity a Muslim practices is acquiring some knowledge and teaching it to his brother." *Ibn Mājah*

26. The Messenger of God ﷺ said, "The most rewarding visitation of the sick is the one that is appropriately brief." *Ad-Daylamī*

20 قَالَ رَسُولُ اللهِ صَلَّى اللهُ عَلَيهِ وَسَلَّمَ: «إِذَا رَأَيْتُمُ الجَنَازَةَ فَقُومُوا لَهَا، حَتَّى تُخْلُفَكُمْ أَو تُوضَعَ» رَوَاهُ البخاري ومسلم

21 قَالَ رَسُولُ اللهِ صَلَّى اللهُ عَلَيهِ وَسَلَّمَ: «ازْهَدْ فِي الدُّنْيَا يُحِبَّكَ اللهُ، وَازهَد فِيمَا عِنْدَ النَّاسِ يُحِبَّكَ النَّاسُ» رَوَاهُ ابن ماجه

22 قَالَ رَسُولُ اللهِ صَلَّى اللهُ عَلَيهِ وَسَلَّمَ: «أُطلُبِ العِلمَ وَلَوْ بِالصِّينِ، فَإِنَّ طَلَبَ العِلْمِ فَرِيضَةٌ عَلَى كُلِّ مُسْلِمٍ»
رَوَاهُ ابن عبد البر

23 قَالَ رَسُولُ اللهِ صَلَّى اللهُ عَلَيهِ وَسَلَّمَ: «اسْتَعِينُوا عَلَى إِنجاحِ الحَوَائِجِ بِالكِتْمَانِ، فَإِنَّ كُلَّ ذِي نِعْمَةٍ مَحْسُودٌ» رَوَاهُ الطبراني

24 قَالَ رَسُولُ اللهِ صَلَّى اللهُ عَلَيهِ وَسَلَّمَ: «أَفضَلُ الفَضَائِلِ أَنْ تَصِلَ مَنْ قَطَعَكَ، وَتُعطِيَ مَنْ حَرَمَكَ، وَتَصْفَحَ عَمَّنْ ظَلَمَكَ» رَوَاهُ الإمام أحمد

25 قَالَ رَسُولُ اللهِ صَلَّى اللهُ عَلَيهِ وَسَلَّمَ: «أَفضَلُ الصَّدَقَةِ أَنْ يَتَعَلَّمَ المَرْءُ المُسْلِمُ عِلْماً، ثُمَّ يُعَلِّمَهُ أَخَاهُ المُسْلِمَ»
رَوَاهُ ابن ماجه

26 قَالَ رَسُولُ اللهِ صَلَّى اللهُ عَلَيهِ وَسَلَّمَ: «أَفْضَلُ العِيَادَةِ أَجْراً سُرْعَةُ القِيَامِ مِنْ عِنْدِ المَرِيْضِ» رَوَاهُ الديلمي

27. The Messenger of God ﷺ said, "True spiritual excellence is devotion to God as if you see Him; and though you do not see Him, you at least know that He sees you." *Al-Bukhārī and Muslim*

28. The Messenger of God ﷺ said, "The worst of heinous sins are idolatry, murder, abuse of one's parents, and false testimony." *Al-Bukhārī*

29. The Messenger of God ﷺ said, "What enables people to enter Paradise more than anything is piety and good character." *At-Tirmidhī*

30. The Messenger of God ﷺ said, "The majority of man's sins emanate from his tongue." *Aṭ-Ṭabarānī*

31. The Messenger of God ﷺ said, "Honor scholars, as they are the inheritors of the prophets. Anyone who honors them has honored God and His Messenger." *Al-Khaṭīb*

32. The Messenger of God ﷺ said, "Reliability enriches, and treachery impoverishes." *Ad-Daylamī*

33. The Messenger of God ﷺ said, "Any heart lacking even a portion of the Qur'an is like a ruined house." *At-Tirmidhī*

27 قَالَ رَسُولُ اللهِ صَلَّى اللهُ عَلَيهِ وَسَلَّمَ: «الإحْسَانُ أَن تَعْبُدَ اللَّهَ كَأَنَّكَ تَرَاهُ، فَإِنْ لَم تَكُنْ تَرَاهُ فَإِنَّهُ يَرَاكَ» رَوَاهُ البخاري ومسلم

28 قَالَ رَسُولُ اللهِ صَلَّى اللهُ عَلَيهِ وَسَلَّمَ: «أَكبَرُ الكَبَائِرِ: الإِشْرَاكُ بِاللهِ، وَقَتْلُ النَّفْسِ، وَعُقُوْقُ الوَالِدَيْنِ وَقَوْلُ الزُّوْرِ» رَوَاهُ البخاري

29 قَالَ رَسُولُ اللهِ صَلَّى اللهُ عَلَيهِ وَسَلَّمَ: «أَكْثَرُ مَا يُدخِلُ الجَنَّةَ تَقْوَى اللهِ وَحُسْنُ الخُلُقِ» رَوَاهُ الترمذي

30 قَالَ رَسُولُ اللهِ صَلَّى اللهُ عَلَيهِ وَسَلَّمَ: «أَكْثَرُ خَطَايَا ابْنِ آدَمَ فِي لِسَانِهِ» رَوَاهُ الطبراني

31 قَالَ رَسُولُ اللهِ صَلَّى اللهُ عَلَيهِ وَسَلَّمَ: «أَكْرِمُوا العُلَمَاءَ، فَإِنَّهُمْ وَرَثَةُ الأَنْبِيَاءِ، فَمَنْ أَكرَمَهُم فقدْ أَكْرَمَ اللهَ وَرَسُولَهُ» رَوَاهُ الخطيب

32 قَالَ رَسُولُ اللهِ صَلَّى اللهُ عَلَيهِ وَسَلَّمَ: «الأَمَانَةُ تَجْلِبُ الرِّزْقَ، وَالخِيَانَةُ تَجْلِبُ الفَقْرَ» رَوَاهُ الديلمي

33 قَالَ رَسُولُ اللهِ صَلَّى اللهُ عَلَيهِ وَسَلَّمَ: «إِنَّ الَّذِي لَيْسَ فِي جَوْفِهِ شَيْءٌ مِنَ القُرْآنِ كَالبَيْتِ الخَرِبِ» رَوَاهُ الترمذي

34. The Messenger of God ﷺ said, "God does not regard your externals or your riches but rather your hearts and your deeds." *Muslim*

35. The Messenger of God ﷺ said, "God is Beautiful and loves beauty." *Muslim*

36. The Messenger of God ﷺ said, "The servants God loves most are those most sincere with God's servants." *Imām Aḥmad*

37. The Messenger of God ﷺ said, "Charity given to one's relatives twice multiplies its reward." *Aṭ-Ṭabarānī*

38. The Messenger of God ﷺ said, "Beware of suspicion, for it is the most deceitful of thought." *Al-Bukhārī and Muslim*

39 The Messenger of God ﷺ said, "Avoid cupidity, for it is instant poverty." *Aṭ-Ṭabarānī*

40. The Messenger of God ﷺ said, "God loves a servant who when performing a task does so skillfully." *Al-Bayhaqī*

41. The Messenger of God ﷺ said, "Modesty is part of faith and fosters only goodness." *Muslim*

34 قَالَ رَسُولُ اللهِ صَلَّى اللهُ عَلَيهِ وَسَلَّمَ: «إِنَّ اللَّهَ لَا يَنْظُرُ إِلَىٰ صُوَرِكُمْ وَأَموَالِكُمْ، وَلكِنْ يَنظُرُ إِلَىٰ قُلُوبِكُمْ وَأَعْمَالِكُمْ» رَوَاهُ مسلم

35 قَالَ رَسُولُ اللهِ صَلَّى اللهُ عَلَيهِ وَسَلَّمَ: «إِنَّ اللَّهَ جَمِيْلٌ يُحِبُّ الجَمَالَ» رَوَاهُ مسلم

36 قَالَ رَسُولُ اللهِ صَلَّى اللهُ عَلَيهِ وَسَلَّمَ: «إِنَّ أَحَبَّ عِبَادِ اللهِ إِلَىٰ اللهِ أَنْصَحُهُمْ لِعِبَادِهِ» رَوَاهُ الإمام أحمد

37 قَالَ رَسُولُ اللهِ صَلَّى اللهُ عَلَيهِ وَسَلَّمَ: «إِنَّ الصَّدَقَةَ عَلَى ذِي قَرَابَةٍ يَضعَّفُ أَجْرُهَا مَرَّتَينِ» رَوَاهُ الطبراني

38 قَالَ رَسُولُ اللهِ صَلَّى اللهُ عَلَيهِ وَسَلَّمَ: «إِيَّاكُمْ وَالظَّنَّ، فَإِنَّ الظَّنَّ أَكْذَبُ الحَدِيْثِ» رَوَاهُ البخاري ومسلم

39 قَالَ رَسُولُ اللهِ صَلَّى اللهُ عَلَيهِ وَسَلَّمَ: «إِيَّاكُمْ وَالطَّمَعَ، فَإِنَّهُ الفَقْرُ الحَاضِرُ» رَوَاهُ الطبراني

40 قَالَ رَسُولُ اللهِ صَلَّى اللهُ عَلَيهِ وَسَلَّمَ: «إِنَّ اللَّهَ يُحِبُّ إِذَا عَمِلَ أَحَدُكُمْ عَمَلاً أَنْ يُتْقِنَهُ» رَوَاهُ البيهقي

41 قَالَ رَسُولُ اللهِ صَلَّى اللهُ عَلَيهِ وَسَلَّمَ: «الحَيَاءُ مِنَ الإِيمَانِ، والحَيَاءُ لَا يَأْتِي إِلَا بِخَيْرٍ» رَوَاهُ مسلم

42. The Messenger of God ﷺ said, "The blessing of food is in washing before and after the meal." *At-Tirmidhī*

43. The Messenger of God ﷺ said, "To acquire some useful knowledge is of greater merit than to perform a hundred devotional prayers voluntarily." *Aṭ-Ṭabarānī*

44. The Messenger of God ﷺ said, "Shake hands, and enmity will fall away; exchange gifts, and mutual love arises." *Imām Mālik*

45. The Messenger of God ﷺ said, "Stay clean as best you can, for God established Islam upon cleanliness." *Ar-Rāfiʿī*

46. The Messenger of God ﷺ said, "Practice humility until no one oppresses or belittles another." *Muslim*

47. The Messenger of God ﷺ said, "Seek out remedies for your ailments, O servants of God, for God has not created a disease without creating a corresponding cure." *Imām Aḥmad*

48. The Messenger of God ﷺ said, "Three practices will keep sincere your brother's love for you: greeting him when you see him; making room for him in gatherings; and calling him by the most endearing of his names." *Al-Bayhaqī*

42 قَالَ رَسُولُ اللهِ صَلَّى اللهُ عَلَيهِ وَسَلَّمَ: «بَرَكَةُ الطَّعَامِ الوُضُوءُ قَبْلَهُ وَالوُضُوءُ بَعْدَهُ» رَوَاهُ الترمذي

43 قَالَ رَسُولُ اللهِ صَلَّى اللهُ عَلَيهِ وَسَلَّمَ: «بَابٌ مِنَ العِلْمِ يَتَعَلَّمُهُ الرَّجُلُ خَيْرٌ لَهُ مِن مِائَةِ رَكْعَةٍ» رَوَاهُ الطبراني

44 قَالَ رَسُولُ اللَّهِ صَلَّى اللَّهِ عَلَيهِ وَسَلَّمَ: «تَصَافَحُوا يَذهَبِ الغِلُّ عَنكُم وَتَهَادُوا تَحَابُّوا» رَوَاهُ الإمام مالك

45 قَالَ رَسُولُ اللهِ صَلَّى اللهُ عَلَيهِ وَسَلَّمَ: «تَنَظَّفُوا بِكُلِّ مَا اسْتَطَعْتُمْ، فَإِنَّ اللهَ تَعَالَى بَنَى الإِسْلَامَ عَلَى النَّظَافَةِ» رَوَاهُ الرّافعي

46 قَالَ رَسُولُ اللهِ صَلَّى اللهُ عَلَيهِ وَسَلَّمَ: «تَوَاضَعُوا حَتَّى لَا يَبْغِيَ أَحَدٌ عَلَى أَحَدٍ، وَلَا يَفْخَرَ أَحَدٌ عَلَى أَحَدٍ» رَوَاهُ مسلم

47 قَالَ رَسُولُ اللهِ صَلَّى اللهُ عَلَيهِ وَسَلَّمَ: «تَدَاوُوا عِبَادَ اللهِ فَإِنَّ اللهَ لَمْ يَضَعْ دَاءً إِلَّا وَضَعَ لَهُ دَوَاءً» رَوَاهُ الإمام أحمد

48 قَالَ رَسُولُ اللهِ صَلَّى اللهُ عَلَيهِ وَسَلَّمَ: «ثَلاثٌ يُصَفِّينَ لَكَ وُدَّ أَخِيكَ: تُسَلِّمُ عَلَيْهِ إِذَا لَقِيتَهُ وَتُوَسِّعُ لَهُ فِي المَجْلِسِ وَتَدْعُوهُ بِأَحَبِّ أَسمَائِهِ إِلَيْهِ» رَوَاهُ البيهقي

49. The Messenger of God ﷺ said, "Three types of people will not enter Paradise: an addict, an abuser of kinship ties, and a believer in magic."[1] *Imām Aḥmad*

50. The Messenger of God ﷺ said, "Paradise lies beneath the feet of mothers." *Imām Aḥmad*

51. The Messenger of God ﷺ said, "Hearts naturally love those who are kind to them and loathe those who are cruel." *Al-Bayhaqī*

52. The Messenger of God ﷺ said, "An older brother's right over his younger siblings is similar to a father's right over his children." *Al-Bayhaqī*

53. The Messenger of God ﷺ said, "Every Muslim has five rights over every other Muslim: the right to a reply, should he greet him; an acceptance, should he invite him; a visit, should he fall ill; a prayer, should he sneeze and praise God; a presence at his funeral, should he die." *Ibn Mājah*

54. The Messenger of God ﷺ said, "Two qualities are never coupled in a believer: miserliness and immorality." *Al-Bukhārī*

55. The Messenger of God ﷺ said, "Set aside what causes you doubt for what does not." *At-Tirmidhī*

49 قَالَ رَسُولُ اللهِ صَلَّى اللهُ عَلَيهِ وَسَلَّمَ: «ثَلَاثَةٌ لَا يَدْخُلُونَ الجَنَّةَ: مُدْمِنُ الخَمْرِ وَقَاطِعُ الرَّحِمِ وَمُصَدِّقٌ بِالسِّحْرِ» رَوَاهُ الإمام أحمد

50 قَالَ رَسُولُ اللهِ صَلَّى اللهُ عَلَيهِ وَسَلَّمَ: «الجَنَّةُ تَحْتَ أَقدَامِ الأُمَّهَاتِ» رَوَاهُ الإمام أحمد

51 قَالَ رَسُولُ اللهِ صَلَّى اللهُ عَلَيهِ وَسَلَّمَ: «جُبِلَتِ القُلُوبُ عَلَى حُبِّ مَنْ أَحسَنَ إِلَيْهَا، وَبُغْضِ مَنْ أَسَاءَ إِلَيْهَا» رَوَاهُ البيهقي

52 قَالَ رَسُولُ اللهِ صَلَّى اللهُ عَلَيهِ وَسَلَّمَ: «حَقُّ كَبِيرِ الإِخْوَةِ عَلَى صَغِيرِهِمْ كَحَقِّ الوَالِدِ عَلَى وَلَدِهِ» رَوَاهُ البيهقي

53 قَالَ رَسُولُ اللهِ صَلَّى اللهُ عَلَيهِ وَسَلَّمَ: «خَمْسٌ مِنْ حَقِّ المُسْلِمِ عَلَى المُسْلِمِ: رَدُّ التَّحِيَّةِ، وَإِجَابَةُ الدَّعْوَةِ، وَشُهُودُ الجَنَازَةِ، وَعِيَادَةُ المَرِيضِ وَتَشْمِيتُ العَاطِسِ إِذَا حَمِدَ اللَّهَ» رَوَاهُ ابن ماجه

54 قَالَ رَسُولُ اللهِ صَلَّى اللهُ عَلَيهِ وَسَلَّمَ: «خَصْلَتَانِ لَا يَجْتَمِعَانِ فِي مُؤْمِنٍ: البُخْلُ وَسُوءُ الخُلُقِ» رَوَاهُ البخاري

55 قَالَ رَسُولُ اللهِ صَلَّى اللهُ عَلَيهِ وَسَلَّمَ: «دَعْ مَا يَرِيْبُكَ إِلىٰ مَا لَا يَرِيْبُكَ» رَوَاهُ الترمذي

56. The Messenger of God ﷺ said, "He who directs others to a good deed is as the one who did it; and, assuredly, God loves the act of aiding the distressed." *Ibn Abī ad-Dunyā*

57. The Messenger of God ﷺ said, "May God have mercy on a servant who spoke well and gained good, or kept silent and avoided harm." *Ibn al-Mubārak*

58. The Messenger of God ﷺ said, "Those who show mercy have God's mercy shown to them. Have mercy on those here on earth, and the One there in Heaven will have mercy on you." *Ibn al-Mubārak and Al-Bayhaqī*

59. The Messenger of God ﷺ said, "Illicit sex begets poverty." *Al-Bayhaqī*

60. The Messenger of God ﷺ said, "Cursing a Muslim is sinful, and murdering him is disbelief." *Al-Bukhārī and Muslim*

61. The Messenger of God ﷺ said, "Say grace; eat with your right hand; and eat what is close at hand." *Al-Bukhārī and Muslim*

62. The Messenger of God ﷺ said, "Prayer is the central pillar of religion." *Al-Bayhaqī*. "Prayer is the key to every good." *Ad-Daylamī*

56 قَالَ رَسُولُ اللهِ صَلَّى اللهُ عَلَيهِ وَسَلَّمَ: «الدَّالُّ عَلَى الخَيْرِ كَفَاعِلِهِ وَاللهُ يُحِبُّ إِغَاثَةَ اللَّهْفَانِ» رَوَاهُ ابن أبي الدنيا

57 قَالَ رَسُولُ اللهِ صَلَّى اللهُ عَلَيهِ وَسَلَّمَ: «رَحِمَ اللهُ عَبْداً قَالَ خَيْراً فَغَنِمَ، أَوْ سَكَتَ عَنْ سُوءٍ فَسَلِمَ» رَوَاهُ ابن المبارك

58 قَالَ رَسُولُ اللهِ صَلَّى اللهُ عَلَيهِ وَسَلَّمَ: «الرَّاحِمُونَ يَرْحَمُهُمُ الرَّحْمٰنُ تَبَارَكَ وَتَعَالَىٰ، ارْحَمُوا مَنْ فِي الأَرْضِ يَرْحَمُكُمْ مَنْ فِي السَّمَاءِ» رَوَاهُ البيهقي وابن المبارك

59 قَالَ رَسُولُ اللهِ صَلَّى اللهُ عَلَيهِ وَسَلَّمَ: «الزِّنَا يُورِثُ الفَقْرَ» رَوَاهُ البيهقي

60 قَالَ رَسُولُ اللهِ صَلَّى اللهُ عَلَيهِ وَسَلَّمَ: «سِبَابُ المُسْلِمِ فُسُوقٌ، وَقِتَالُهُ كُفْرٌ» رَوَاهُ البخاري ومسلم

61 قَالَ رَسُولُ اللهِ صَلَّى اللهُ عَلَيهِ وَسَلَّمَ: «سَمِّ اللهَ، وَكُلْ بِيَمِينِكَ، وَكُلْ مِمَّا يَلِيْكَ» رَوَاهُ البخاري ومسلم

62 قَالَ رَسُولُ اللهِ صَلَّى اللهُ عَلَيهِ وَسَلَّمَ: «الصَّلاةُ عِمَادُ الدِّينِ» رَوَاهُ البيهقي «الصَّلاةُ مِفتاحُ كُلِّ خَيرٍ» رَوَاهُ الديلمي

63. The Messenger of God ﷺ said, "Prayer in congregation surpasses individual prayer by twenty-seven degrees." *Al-Bukhārī and Muslim*

64. The Messenger of God ﷺ said, "Fast, and flourish." *Aṭ-Ṭabarānī*

65. The Messenger of God ﷺ said, "One beneficial scholar is better than a thousand worshipful devotees." *Ad-Daylamī*

66. The Messenger of God ﷺ said, "Consider well contentment, for it is a treasure without end." *Aṭ-Ṭabarānī*

67. The Messenger of God ﷺ said, "A kind word is charity." *Al-Bukhārī and Muslim*

68. The Messenger of God ﷺ said, "A person has done enough wrong in his life if he simply repeats everything he hears." *Abū Dāwūd*

69. The Messenger of God ﷺ said, "God censures women who frequent graves as well as those who take them as prayer sites or settees." *At-Tirmidhī*

70. The Messenger of God ﷺ said, "God condemns the one who takes, pays, witnesses, or notarizes a usurious transaction." *Abū Dāwūd*

63 قَالَ رَسُولُ اللهِ صَلَّى اللهُ عَلَيهِ وَسَلَّمَ: «صَلاةُ الجَمَاعَةِ تَفضُلُ صَلاةَ الفَذِّ بِسَبعٍ وَعِشْرِينَ دَرَجَةً» رَوَاهُ البخاري ومسلم

64 قَالَ رَسُولُ اللهِ صَلَّى اللهُ عَلَيهِ وَسَلَّمَ: «صُومُوا تَصِحُّوا» رَوَاهُ الطبراني

65 قَالَ رَسُولُ اللهِ صَلَّى اللهُ عَلَيهِ وَسَلَّمَ: «عَالِمٌ يُنْتَفَعُ بِهِ خَيْرٌ مِنْ أَلْفِ عَابِدٍ» رَوَاهُ الديلمي

66 قَالَ رَسُولُ اللهِ صَلَّى اللهُ عَلَيهِ وَسَلَّمَ: «عَلَيْكُمْ بِالقَنَاعَةِ، فَإِنَّ القَنَاعَةَ مَالٌ لَا يَنْفَدُ» رَوَاهُ الطبراني

67 قَالَ رَسُولُ اللهِ صَلَّى اللهُ عَلَيهِ وَسَلَّمَ: «الكَلِمَةُ الطَّيِّبَةُ صَدَقَةٌ» رَوَاهُ البخاري ومسلم

68 قَالَ رَسُولُ اللهِ صَلَّى اللهُ عَلَيهِ وَسَلَّمَ: «كَفَى بِالمَرْءِ إِثْماً أَنْ يُحَدِّثَ بِكُلِّ مَا سَمِعَ» رَوَاهُ أبو داود

69 قَالَ رَسُولُ اللهِ صَلَّى اللهُ عَلَيهِ وَسَلَّمَ: «لَعَنَ اللهُ زَائِرَاتِ القُبُورِ وَالمُتَّخِذِينَ عَلَيْهَا المَسَاجِدَ وَالسُّرُجَ» رَوَاهُ الترمذي

70 قَالَ رَسُولُ اللهِ صَلَّى اللهُ عَلَيهِ وَسَلَّمَ: «لَعَنَ اللهُ آكِلَ الرِبَا وَمُوكِلَهُ وَشَاهِدَهُ وَكَاتِبَهُ» رَوَاهُ أبو داود

71. The Messenger of God ﷺ said, "God condemns a man who dresses like a woman or a woman who dresses like a man." *Al-Ḥākim*

72. The Messenger of God ﷺ said, "A believer is not one who eats his fill while his next door neighbor goes hungry." *Al-Bayhaqī*

73. The Messenger of God ﷺ said, "Whoever fails to care for our youth, respect our aged, enjoin right, and denounce wrong is not counted among us." *At-Tirmidhī and Imām Aḥmad*

74. The Messenger of God ﷺ said, "A young man never honors an old man due to age but that God sends someone to honor him when he reaches that age." *At-Tirmidhī*

75. The Messenger of God ﷺ said, "God has never dignified anyone due to his ignorance, nor humiliated anyone due to his forbearance. And wealth is never diminished as a result of charity." *Ad-Daylamī*

76. The Messenger of God ﷺ said, "A Muslim never gives a fellow Muslim a better gift than wisdom through which God increases him in guidance or turns him away from harmful behavior." *Al-Bayhaqī*

77. The Messenger of God ﷺ said, "If a Muslim consoles his brother during some crisis, God will adorn him in garments of grace on the Day of Judgment." *Ibn Mājah*

71 قَالَ رَسُولُ اللهِ صَلَّى اللهُ عَلَيهِ وَسَلَّمَ: «لَعَنَ اللهُ الرَّجُلَ يَلْبَسُ لِبْسَةَ المَرأَةِ، وَالمَرأَةَ تَلبَسُ لِبْسَةَ الرَّجُلِ» رَوَاهُ الحاكم

72 قَالَ رَسُولُ اللهِ صَلَّى اللهُ عَلَيهِ وَسَلَّمَ: «لَيْسَ المُؤمِنُ بِالَّذِي يَشْبَعُ وَجَارُهُ إِلىٰ جَنْبِهِ جَائِعٌ» رَوَاهُ البيهقي

73 قَالَ رَسُولُ اللهِ صَلَّى اللهُ عَلَيهِ وَسَلَّمَ: «لَيْسَ مِنَّا مَنْ لم يَرْحَمْ صَغِيْرَنَا وَيُوَقِّرْ كَبِيْرَنَا، وَيَأْمُرْ بِالمَعْرُوفِ وَيَنْهَ عَنِ المُنْكَرِ» رَوَاهُ الترمذي والإمام أحمد

74 قَالَ رَسُولُ اللهِ صَلَّى اللهُ عَلَيهِ وَسَلَّمَ: «مَا أَكرَمَ شَابٌّ شَيْخاً لِسِنِّهِ إِلَّا قَيَّضَ اللهُ مَنْ يُكْرِمُهُ عِنْدَ سِنِّه» رَوَاهُ الترمذي

75 قَالَ رَسُولُ اللهِ صَلَّى اللهُ عَلَيهِ وَسَلَّمَ: «مَا أَعزَّ اللهُ بِجَهْلٍ قَطُّ، وَلا أَذَلَّ بِحِلْمٍ قَطُّ وَلاَ نَقَصَتْ صَدَقَةٌ مِنْ مَالٍ» رَوَاهُ الديلمي

76 قَالَ رَسُولُ اللهِ صَلَّى اللهُ عَلَيهِ وَسَلَّمَ: «مَا أَهْدَى المَرْءُ المُسْلِمُ لَأخِيْهِ هَدِيَّةً أَفْضَلَ مِنْ كَلِمَةِ حِكْمَةٍ يَزِيْدُهُ اللهُ بِهَا هُدًى أَوْ يَرُدُّهُ بِهَا عَنْ رَدًى» رَوَاهُ البيهقي

77 قَالَ رَسُولُ اللهِ صَلَّى اللهُ عَلَيهِ وَسَلَّمَ: «مَا مِنْ مُسْلِمٍ يُعَزِّي أَخَاهُ فِي مُصِيْبَةٍ، إِلَّا كَسَاهُ اللهُ مِنْ حُلَلِ الكَرَامَةِ يَوْمَ القِيَامَةِ» رَوَاهُ ابن ماجه

78. The Messenger of God ﷺ said, "The prayers of one who seeks guidance from a psychic will not be accepted for forty days." *Muslim*

79. The Messenger of God ﷺ said, "Whosoever adds to this matter of ours what is alien to it will have it rejected." *Al-Bukhārī*

80. The Messenger of God ﷺ said, "Whoever attempts to fault a man by mentioning something untrue about him will be detained in Hell by God until he produces the proof for his remarks." *Aṭ-Ṭabarānī*

81. The Messenger of God ﷺ said, "Veiling the faults of the faithful is akin to restoring life to the dead." *Aṭ-Ṭabarānī*

82. The Messenger of God ﷺ said, "On the Day of Judgment, God will humiliate and forsake anyone who betrays a believer to a tyrant." *Al-Bayhaqī*

83. The Messenger of God ﷺ said, "Whoever defrauds us is not one of us; deception and guile are hellish." *Abū Dāwūd* and *Aṭ-Ṭabarānī*

84. The Messenger of God ﷺ said, "God veils the faults of anyone who suppresses his anger." *Ibn Abī ad-Dunyā*

78 قَالَ رَسُولُ اللهِ صَلَّى اللهُ عَلَيهِ وَسَلَّمَ: «مَنْ أَتَى عَرَّافاً فَسَأَلَهُ عَنْ شَيءٍ لَمْ تُقْبَلْ لَهُ صَلاَةٌ أَربَعِيْنَ يَوْماً» رَوَاهُ مسلم

79 قَالَ رَسُولُ اللهِ صَلَّى اللهُ عَلَيهِ وَسَلَّمَ: «مَنْ أَحْدَثَ فِي أَمْرِنَا هَذَا مَا لَيْسَ مِنْهُ فَهُوَ رَدٌّ» رَوَاهُ البخاري

80 قَالَ رَسُولُ اللهِ صَلَّى اللهُ عَلَيهِ وَسَلَّمَ: «مَن ذَكَرَ امْرَأً بِمَا لَيْسَ فِيْهِ لِيَعِيْبَهُ حَبَسَهُ اللهُ فِي نَارِ جَهَنَّمَ حَتَّى يَأتِيَ بِنَفَاذِ مَا قَالَ» رَوَاهُ الطبراني

81 قَالَ رَسُولُ اللهِ صَلَّى اللهُ عَلَيهِ وَسَلَّمَ: «مَنْ سَتَرَ عَلَى مُؤْمِنٍ عَوْرَةً، فَكَأَنَّمَا أَحْيَا مَيِّتاً» رَوَاهُ الطبراني

82 قَالَ رَسُولُ اللهِ صَلَّى اللهُ عَلَيهِ وَسَلَّمَ: «مَنْ سَعَى بِمُؤْمِنٍ أَقَامَهُ اللهُ مَقَامَ ذُلٍّ وَخِزْيٍ يَوْمَ القِيَامَةِ» رَوَاهُ البيهقي

83 قَالَ رَسُولُ اللهِ صَلَّى اللهُ عَلَيهِ وَسَلَّمَ: «مَنْ غَشَّنَا فَلَيسَ مِنَّا، وَالمَكْرُ وَالخِدَاعُ فِي النَّارِ» رَوَاهُ الطبراني وأبو داود لفظه «وَالمَكْرُ وَالخَدِيعَةُ وَالخِيَانَةُ فِي النَّارِ»

84 قَالَ رَسُولُ اللهِ صَلَّى اللهُ عَلَيهِ وَسَلَّمَ: «مَنْ كَفَّ غَضَبَهُ سَتَرَ اللهُ عَوْرَتَهُ» رَوَاهُ ابن أبي الدنيا

85. The Messenger of God ﷺ said, "Whoever walks with a tyrant in support of him, while aware of his tyranny, has abandoned Islam." *Aṭ-Ṭabarānī*

86. The Messenger of God ﷺ said, "Whoever has no shame before others has no shame before God." *Aṭ-Ṭabarānī*

87. The Messenger of God ﷺ said, "The Muslim is one from whose tongue and hand other Muslims are safe." *Al-Bukhārī and Muslim*

88. The Messenger of God ﷺ said, "Muslims are a fraternity; therefore, there is no superiority of one over another, except in scruples." *Aṭ-Ṭabarānī*

89. The Messenger of God ﷺ said, "If a man's actions slow him down, his good name will not speed him up." *Muslim*

90. The Messenger of God ﷺ said, "A person's spiritual practice is only as good as that of his close friends; so consider well whom you befriend." *At-Tirmidhī*

91. The Messenger of God ﷺ said, "Never express joy at your fellow man's afflictions, for God just might free him of them and afflict you." *Aṭ-Ṭabarānī*

85 قَالَ رَسُولُ اللهِ صَلَّى اللهُ عَلَيهِ وَسَلَّمَ: «مَنْ مَشَى مَعَ ظَالِمٍ لِيُعِيْنَهُ وَهُوَ يَعلَمُ أنَّهُ ظَالِمٌ فَقَدْ خَرَجَ مِنَ الإِسْلَامِ»
رَوَاهُ الطبراني

86 قَالَ رَسُولُ اللهِ صَلَّى اللهُ عَلَيهِ وَسَلَّمَ: «مَنْ لَا يَسْتَحِي مِنَ النَّاسِ لَا يَسْتَحِي مِنَ اللهِ» رَوَاهُ الطبراني

87 قَالَ رَسُولُ اللهِ صَلَّى اللهُ عَلَيهِ وَسَلَّمَ: « المُسْلِمُ مَنْ سَلِمَ المُسلِمُونَ مِنْ لِسَانِهِ وَيَدِهِ» رَوَاهُ البخاري ومسلم

88 قَالَ رَسُولُ اللهِ صَلَّى اللهُ عَلَيهِ وَسَلَّمَ: «المُسلِمُونَ إخْوَةٌ، لا فَضْلَ لِأَحَدٍ عَلَى أَحَدٍ إِلَّا بِالتَّقْوَى» رَوَاهُ الطبراني

89 قَالَ رَسُولُ اللهِ صَلَّى اللهُ عَلَيهِ وَسَلَّمَ: «مَنْ أَبْطَأَ بِهِ عَمَلُهُ، لَمْ يُسْرِعْ بِهِ حَسَبُهُ» رَوَاهُ مسلم

90 قَالَ رَسُولُ اللهِ صَلَّى اللهُ عَلَيهِ وَسَلَّمَ: «المَرْءُ عَلَى دِينِ خَلِيْلِهِ، فَلْيَنْظُرْ أَحَدُكُمْ مَنْ يُخَالِلُ» رَوَاهُ الترمذي

91 قَالَ رَسُولُ اللهِ صَلَّى اللهُ عَلَيهِ وَسَلَّمَ: «لَا تُظْهِرِ الشَّمَاتَةَ لِأَخِيْكَ فَيَرحَمَهُ اللهُ وَيَبْتَلِيَكَ» رَوَاهُ الطبراني

92. The Messenger of God ﷺ said, "Whoever cannot be trusted has no faith, and whoever breaches contracts has no religion." *Imām Aḥmad*

93. The Messenger of God ﷺ said, "Do not belittle any act of kindness, even that of greeting your brother with a cheerful countenance." *Muslim*

94. The Messenger of God ﷺ said, "A man should never sit between two persons unless granted their permission." *Abū Dāwūd*

95. The Messenger of God ﷺ said, "Do not follow a funeral procession shouting or with displays of fire." *Abū Dāwūd*

96. The Messenger of God ﷺ said, "God loves to see His servant exhausted after an honest day's work." *Ad-Daylamī*

97. The Messenger of God ﷺ said, "Recall the good qualities of your dead, and refrain from mentioning their shortcomings." *At-Tirmidhī*

98. The Messenger of God ﷺ said, "Do not drink liquor, for it is the key to every evil." *Ibn Mājah*

99. The Messenger of God ﷺ said, "Never strike your maids over broken dishes, for dishes, like people, have predetermined life spans." *Abū Nuʿaym*

92 قَالَ رَسُولُ اللهِ صَلَّى اللهُ عَلَيهِ وَسَلَّمَ: «لَا إِيمَانَ لِمَنْ لَا أَمَانَةَ لَهُ، وَلَا دِيْنَ لِمَنْ لَا عَهْدَ لَهُ» رَوَاهُ الإمام أحمد

93 قَالَ رَسُولُ اللهِ صَلَّى اللهُ عَلَيهِ وَسَلَّمَ: «لَا تَحْقِرَنَّ مِنَ المَعرُوْفِ شَيْئاً وَلَوْ أَنْ تَلْقَى أَخَاكَ بِوَجْهٍ طَلِقٍ» رَوَاهُ مسلم

94 قَالَ رَسُولُ اللهِ صَلَّى اللهُ عَلَيهِ وَسَلَّمَ: «لَا يَجْلِسُ الرَّجُلُ بَيْنَ اثْنَيْنِ إِلَّا بِإِذْنِهِمَا» رَوَاهُ أبو داود

95 قَالَ رَسُولُ اللهِ صَلَّى اللهُ عَلَيهِ وَسَلَّمَ: «لَا تُتْبَعُ الجَنَازَةُ بِصَوْتٍ وَلَا نَارٍ» رَوَاهُ أبو داود

96 قَالَ رَسُولُ اللهِ صَلَّى اللهُ عَلَيهِ وَسَلَّمَ: «إِنَّ اللهَ يُحِبُّ أَنْ يَرَى عَبْدَهُ تَعِباً فِي طَلَبِ الحَلَالِ» رَوَاهُ الديلمي

97 قَالَ رَسُولُ اللهِ صَلَّى اللهُ عَلَيهِ وَسَلَّمَ: «اذكُرُوا مَحَاسِنَ مَوْتَاكُمْ وَكُفُّوا عَنْ مَسَاوِيْهِمْ» رَوَاهُ الترمذي

98 قَالَ رَسُولُ اللهِ صَلَّى اللهُ عَلَيهِ وَسَلَّمَ: «لَا تَشْرَبُوا الخَمْرَ فَإِنَّهَا مِفْتَاحُ كُلِّ شَرٍّ» رَوَاهُ ابن ماجه

99 قَالَ رَسُولُ اللهِ صَلَّى اللهُ عَلَيهِ وَسَلَّمَ: «لَا تَضْرِبُوا إِمَاءَكُمْ عَلَى كَسْرِ إِنَائِكُمْ فَإِنَّ لَهَا آجَالاً كَآجَالِ النَّاسِ» رَوَاهُ أبو نعيم

100. The Messenger of God ﷺ said, “Neither argue with nor tease your brother, and never give your word to him and then break it.” *At-Tirmidhī*

101. The Messenger of God ﷺ said, “It is prohibited for a Muslim to frighten another Muslim.” *Abū Dāwūd*

102. The Messenger of God ﷺ said, “God’s protective hand is with the congregation.” *At-Tirmidhī*

103. The Messenger of God ﷺ said, “The most complete in faith are those best in character and kindest to their families.” *At-Tirmidhī*

104. The Messenger of God ﷺ said, “Anytime you lighten the load of your servant, a reward is allotted to your scales on the Day of Judgment.” *Al-Bayhaqī*

105. The Messenger of God ﷺ said, “Speak the truth even though it be bitter.” *Ibn Ḥibbān*

106. Whenever the Messenger of God ﷺ sneezed, he would place his hand or a handkerchief over his mouth to stifle the sound. *Al-Ḥākim*

107. The Messenger of God ﷺ said, “Fulfillment is not plenty of goods; rather, it is self-fulfillment.” *Al-Bukhārī and Muslim*

100 قَالَ رَسُولُ اللهِ صَلَّى اللهُ عَلَيهِ وَسَلَّمَ: «لا تُمَارِ أَخَاكَ وَلَا تُمَازِحْهُ، وَلَا تَعِدْهُ مَوْعِداً فَتُخْلِفَهُ» رَوَاهُ الترمذي

101 قَالَ رَسُولُ اللهِ صَلَّى اللهُ عَلَيهِ وَسَلَّمَ: «لا يَحِلُّ لِمُسْلِمٍ أَنْ يُرَوِّعَ مُسْلِماً» رَوَاهُ أبو داود

102 قَالَ رَسُولُ اللهِ صَلَّى اللهُ عَلَيهِ وَسَلَّمَ: «يَدُ اللهِ مَعَ الجَمَاعَةِ» رَوَاهُ الترمذي

103 قَالَ رَسُولُ اللهِ صَلَّى اللهُ عَلَيهِ وَسَلَّمَ: «أَكْمَلُ المُؤْمِنِينَ إِيْمَاناً أَحْسَنُهُمْ خُلُقاً وَأَلْطَفُهُمْ لِأَهْلِهِ» رَوَاهُ الترمذي

104 قَالَ رَسُولُ اللهِ صَلَّى اللهُ عَلَيهِ وَسَلَّمَ: «مَا خَفَّفْتَ عَنْ خَادِمِكَ مِنْ عَمَلِهِ فَهُوَ أَجرٌ لَكَ فِي مَوَازِيْنِكَ يَوْمَ القِيَامَةِ» رَوَاهُ البيهقي

105 قَالَ رَسُولُ اللهِ صَلَّى اللهُ عَلَيهِ وَسَلَّمَ: «قُلِ الحَقَّ وَإِنْ كَانَ مُرّاً» رَوَاهُ ابن حبان

106 كَانَ رَسُولُ اللهِ صَلَّى اللهُ عَلَيْهِ وَسَلَّمَ إِذَا عَطَسَ وَضَعَ يَدَهُ أَو ثَوبَهُ عَلَى فِيْهِ وَخَفَضَ بِهَا صَوْتَهُ. رَوَاهُ الحاكم

107 قَالَ رَسُولُ اللهِ صَلَّى اللهُ عَلَيهِ وَسَلَّمَ: «لَيْسَ الغِنَى عَنْ كَثْرَةِ العَرَضِ، وَلكِنَّ الغِنَى غِنَى النَّفْسِ» رَوَاهُ البخاري ومسلم

108. The Messenger of God ﷺ said, “Gentleness never accompanies anything without enhancing it, nor is it ever removed from anything without demeaning it.” *Al-Bayhaqī*

109. God’s Messenger ﷺ never confronted people directly with anything reprehensible to them. *Imām Aḥmad*

110. The Messenger of God ﷺ said, “Never do in private what you would conceal from others in public.” *Ibn Mājah*

111. The Messenger of God ﷺ said, “No one has eaten better food than the one who eats from the labor of his own hands.” *Al-Bukhārī*

112. The Messenger of God ﷺ said, “A parent can give a child no greater gift than beautiful manners.” *Al-Ḥākim*

113. The Messenger of God ﷺ said, “Condemned is the sodomite for his sodomy.” *Imām Aḥmad*

114. The Messenger of God ﷺ said, “Condemned is anyone who separates child from mother.” *Al-Bayhaqī*

115. The Messenger of God ﷺ said, “Beautiful Islam entails minding one’s own business.” *At-Tirmidhī*

108 قَالَ رَسُولُ اللهِ صَلَّى اللهُ عَلَيهِ وَسَلَّمَ: «مَا كَانَ الرِّفْقُ فِي شَيءٍ إِلَّا زَانَهُ، وَمَا نُزِعَ مِنْ شَيءٍ إِلَّا شَانَهُ» رَوَاهُ البيهقي

109 كانَ رَسُولُ اللهِ صَلَّى اللهُ عَلَيهِ وَسَلَّمَ لَا يُوَاجِهُ أَحداً فِي وَجْهِهِ بِشَيْءٍ يَكْرَهُهُ. رَوَاهُ الإمام أحمد

110 قَالَ رَسُولُ اللهِ صَلَّى اللهُ عَلَيهِ وَسَلَّمَ: «مَا كَرِهْتَ أَنْ يَرَاهُ النَّاسُ مِنْكَ فَلَا تَفْعَلهُ بِنَفْسِكَ إِذَا خَلَوْتَ» رَوَاهُ ابن ماجه

111 قَالَ رَسُولُ اللهِ صَلَّى اللهُ عَلَيهِ وَسَلَّمَ: «مَا أَكَلَ أَحَدٌ طَعَاماً قَطُّ خَيْراً مِنْ أَنْ يَأْكُلَ مِن عَمَلِ يَدِهِ» رَوَاهُ البخاري

112 قَالَ رَسُولُ اللهِ صَلَّى اللهُ عَلَيهِ وَسَلَّمَ: «مَا نَحلَ وَالِدٌ وَلَدَهُ أَفْضَلَ مِنْ أَدَبٍ حَسَنٍ» رَوَاهُ الحاكم

113 قَالَ رَسُولُ اللهِ صَلَّى اللهُ عَلَيهِ وَسَلَّمَ: «مَلْعُونٌ مَنْ عَمِلَ بِعَمَلِ قَوْمِ لُوطٍ» رَوَاهُ الإمام أحمد

114 قَالَ رَسُولُ اللهِ صَلَّى اللهُ عَلَيهِ وَسَلَّمَ: «مَلعُونٌ مَنْ فَرَّقَ بَيْنَ وَالِدَةٍ وَوَلَدِهَا» رَوَاهُ البيهقي

115 قَالَ رَسُولُ اللهِ صَلَّى اللهُ عَلَيهِ وَسَلَّمَ: «مِنْ حُسْنِ إِسْلَامِ الـمَرْءِ تَرْكُهُ مَا لا يَعْنِيهِ» رَوَاهُ الترمذي

116. The Messenger of God ﷺ said, "Whoever decides to relocate solely to study sacred knowledge is forgiven before even setting out." *At-Tirmidhī*

117. The Messenger of God ﷺ said, "Whoever does you a favor, repay him; and if you are unable to, then at least pray for him." *Aṭ-Ṭabarānī*

118. The Messenger of God ﷺ said, "Whoever eats pure food, acts with prophetic scruples, and secures others from his own misfortunes shall enter Paradise." *At-Tirmidhī*

119. The Messenger of God ﷺ said, "A person who teaches goodness to others while neglecting his own soul is like an oil lamp, which illumines others while burning itself out." *Aṭ-Ṭabarānī*

120. The Messenger of God ﷺ said, "He who sins laughing enters Hell crying." *Abū Nuʿaym*

121. The Messenger of God ﷺ said, "God enriches the thrifty and impoverishes the spendthrift; God elevates the humble and whoever tyrannizes others, God will crush him." *Al-Bazār*

122. The Messenger of God ﷺ said, "Whoever pleases his parents has pleased God, and whoever angers them has angered God." *Ibn an-Najjār*

116 قَالَ رَسُولُ اللهِ صَلَّى اللهُ عَلَيهِ وَسَلَّمَ: «مَنِ انتَقَلَ لِيَتَعَلَّمَ العِلْمَ غُفِرَ لَهُ قَبْلَ أَنْ يَخْطُوَ» رَوَاهُ الترمذي

117 قَالَ رَسُولُ اللهِ صَلَّى اللهُ عَلَيهِ وَسَلَّمَ: «مَنْ أَتَى إِلَيْكُمْ مَعْرُوفاً فَكَافِئُوهُ، فَإِنْ لَمْ تَجِدُوا فَادْعُوا لَهُ» رَوَاهُ الطبراني

118 قَالَ رَسُولُ اللهِ صَلَّى اللهُ عَلَيهِ وَسَلَّمَ: «مَنْ أَكَلَ طَيِّباً، وَعَمِلَ فِي سُنَّةٍ، وَأَمِنَ النَّاسُ بَوَائِقَهُ، دَخَلَ الجَنَّةَ» رَوَاهُ الترمذي

119 قَالَ رَسُولُ اللهِ صَلَّى اللهُ عَلَيهِ وَسَلَّمَ: «مَثَلُ الَّذِي يُعَلِّمُ النَّاسَ الخَيْرَ وَيَنْسَى نَفْسَهُ كَمَثَلِ السِّرَاجِ يُضِيءُ لِلنَّاسِ وَيَحْرِقُ نَفْسَهُ» رَوَاهُ الطبراني

120 قَالَ رَسُولُ اللهِ صَلَّى اللهُ عَلَيهِ وَسَلَّمَ: «مَنْ أَذنَبَ وَهُوَ يَضْحَكُ، دَخَلَ النَّارَ وَهُوَ يَبْكِي» رَوَاهُ أبو نعيم

121 قَالَ رَسُولُ اللهِ صَلَّى اللهُ عَلَيهِ وَسَلَّمَ: «مَنِ اقْتَصَدَ أَغنَاهُ اللهُ، وَمَنْ بَذَّرَ أَفقَرَهُ اللهُ، وَمَنْ تَوَاضَعَ رَفَعَهُ اللهُ، وَمَنْ تَجَبَّرَ قَصَمَهُ اللهُ» رَوَاهُ البزار

122 قَالَ رَسُولُ اللهِ صَلَّى اللهُ عَلَيهِ وَسَلَّمَ: «مَنْ أَرضَى وَالِدَيْهِ فَقَدْ أَرْضَى اللَّهَ، وَمَنْ أَسخَطَ وَالِدَيْهِ فَقَدْ أَسْخَطَ اللَّهَ» رَوَاهُ ابن النجار

123. The Messenger of God ﷺ said, "Anyone who sees a believer degraded, and, being able to defend him, does not, is degraded by God on the Day of Judgment." *Imām Aḥmad*

124. The Messenger of God ﷺ said, "One aspect of manliness is for a fellow to listen attentively to his brother should he address him." *Al-Khaṭīb*

125. The Messenger of God ﷺ said, "Whoever spies on a group's private conversation knowing they would dislike him doing so shall have lead poured into his ears on the Day of Judgment." *Al-Bukhārī*

126. The Messenger of God ﷺ said, "Whoever faults his brother for some wrong shall not die before doing it himself." *At-Tirmidhī*

127. The Messenger of God ﷺ said, "Whoever counsels his brother to take a certain course, while knowing that a better course lies elsewhere, has in essence betrayed him." *Abū Dāwūd*

128. The Messenger of God ﷺ said, "Whoever uses sophistical arguments knowingly continues to be the object of God's wrath until he desists." *Abū Dāwūd*

129. The Messenger of God ﷺ said, "God removes faith from one who engages in illicit sex or consumes intoxicants just as a man removes his shirt when pulling it over his head." *Al-Ḥākim*

123 قَالَ رَسُولُ اللهِ صَلَّى اللهُ عَلَيهِ وَسَلَّمَ: «مَنْ أُذِلَّ عِنْدَهُ مُؤْمِنٌ فَلَمْ يَنْصُرْهُ وَهُوَ يَقْدِرُ عَلَى أَنْ يَنْصُرَهُ، أَذَلَّهُ اللهُ يَوْمَ القِيَامَةِ» رَوَاهُ الإمام أحمد

124 قَالَ رَسُولُ اللهِ صَلَّى اللهُ عَلَيهِ وَسَلَّمَ: «مِنَ الـمُرُوءَةِ أَنْ يُنْصِتَ الأَخُ لِأَخِيْهِ إِذَا حَدَّثَهُ» رَوَاهُ الخطيب

125 قَالَ رَسُولُ اللهِ صَلَّى اللهُ عَلَيهِ وَسَلَّمَ: «مَنْ تَسَمَّعَ حَدِيْثَ قَوْمٍ وَهُمْ لَهُ كَارِهُونَ صُبَّ فِي أُذُنَيْهِ الآنُكُ يَوْمَ القِيَامَةِ» رَوَاهُ البخاري

126 قَالَ رَسُولُ اللهِ صَلَّى اللهُ عَلَيهِ وَسَلَّمَ: «مَنْ عَيَّرَ أَخَاهُ بِذَنْبٍ لَم يَمُتْ حَتَّى يَعْمَلَهُ» رَوَاهُ الترمذي

127 قَالَ رَسُولُ اللهِ صَلَّى اللهُ عَلَيهِ وَسَلَّمَ: «مَنْ أَشَارَ عَلَى أَخِيْهِ بِأَمْرٍ يَعْلَمُ أَنَّ الرُّشْدَ فِي غَيْرِهِ فَقَدْ خَانَهُ» رَوَاهُ أبو داود

128 قَالَ رَسُولُ اللهِ صَلَّى اللهُ عَلَيهِ وَسَلَّمَ: «مَنْ خَاصَمَ فِي بَاطِلٍ وَهُوَ يَعلَمُ لَمْ يَزَلْ فِي سَخَطِ اللهِ حَتَّى يَنْزِعَ» رَوَاهُ أبو داود

129 قَالَ رَسُولُ اللهِ صَلَّى اللهُ عَلَيهِ وَسَلَّمَ: «مَنْ زَنَى أَو شَرِبَ الخَمْرَ نَزَعَ اللهُ مِنْهُ الإيمَانَ كَمَا يَخْلَعُ القَمِيْصَ مِنْ رَأْسِهِ» رَوَاهُ الحاكم

130. The Messenger of God ﷺ said, "Whoever visits a soothsayer or a diviner and believes what he is told has disbelieved in what was revealed to Muḥammad ﷺ."
*Imām Aḥmad*

NOTES

1 Scholars have mentioned that this does not imply they will forever be denied Paradise, but that they are not among those who enter without purgatory.

130 قَالَ رَسُولُ اللهِ صَلَّى اللهُ عَلَيهِ وَسَلَّمَ: «مَنْ أَتَى عَرَّافاً أَو كَاهِناً
وَصَدَّقَهُ بِمَا يَقُولُ فَقَدْ كَفَرَ بِمَا أُنزِلَ عَلَى مُحَمَّدٍ»
رَوَاهُ الإمام أحمد

# Translator's Note

## HADITH CLASSIFICATIONS

Hadith literature, which consists largely of the sayings and deeds of the Prophet Muhammad ﷺ, together with descriptions of his character and behavior, is both rich and vast. Sadly, the majority of the Prophet's sayings have not been translated into English, and of the translations that have been made, many are either inadequate or outdated. Recently, however, many native English speakers, born and bred in the West but trained in the traditional lands of Islam, are beginning to translate hadith. This is indeed a bright development in a neglected field. While the perils are great, due to the loftiness of the subject and the immense weight of responsibility, the need has never been greater.

This collection was given to me by a young East African student of one of my own teachers, Ḥabīb Aḥmad Mashhūr al-Ḥaddād, may God sanctify his secret. The student visited me in California and explained to me the need for such a work in English and the immense impact the collection had on his native country in East Africa. He kindly parted with his only copy and left it in my possession where it remained for some time. One morning, I decided to begin the day by translating five hadith from the collection. I ended up spending the entire day translating the complete work and spending several weeks thereafter reworking the translation.

At a certain point, a translator feels the treachery of translation, the impossibility of it, but carries on for the importance of the attempt. There are many ways to turn a phrase, but even to hint at the sublime and succinct Arabic of the Prophet ﷺ is not in this mere mortal's capacity. I have tried my best, and I hope readers benefit from this translation as much as have the readers of the Swahili version of the sayings.

## ABOUT HADITH LITERATURE

To aid the beginning reader, I would like to clarify a few points about the rating of hadith literature. Hadith are classified according to their "strength," which means their probability of being accurate transmissions of the Prophet's actual words, deeds, and character. The science of hadith classification, which emerged in the late first century AH due to the number of fabricated hadith that were spreading among the Muslims, is very precise and surprisingly modern and rigorous. It judges hadith according to many sophisticated criteria, including the number and verifiability of their chains of transmission from the original narrators, and it rates them as sound, good, or weak (*ṣaḥīḥ*, *ḥasan*, or *ḍaʿīf*). Although many Orientalists have attempted to attack the veracity of hadith literature due to its reliance on human memory, they only succeed in exposing their own ignorance. To those who have taken the study seriously and have been blessed with hearing narrations from certified experts with prodigious memories that can perform exact recall, the reliability of both the transmissions and the classifications is remarkable.

As the Arabs say, "He who sees a wonder and he who hears of it are not the same." The living masters of today, who still memorize vast numbers of hadith, confirm undoubtedly the testimonies of previous generations concerning the memories of men such as Imām al-Bukhārī. I personally had the benefit of spending time with a scholar from Mauritania who had memorized, with chains of narration, the entire nine canonical hadith collections. This means that he had memorized literally tens of thousands of hadith, along with hundreds of thousands of the narrators' names.

The reader will note that this edition includes the biographies of the narrators of the hadith in this collection, since their identities, reputations, and capabilities are crucial to the chain of narration.

## CATEGORIES OF HADITH

Beyond the three basic classifications (sound, good, and weak), there are dozens (some would argue hundreds) of sub-categories. The soundest hadith of all are the reports transmitted through multiple chains (*mutawātir*). These are considered analogous to incontestable factual information, such as the existence of Australia though we may never have been there or historical accounts that are undeniable, such as the Norman invasion of England in 1066. Less than a thousand hadith have achieved this status. These are undeniably the words of the Prophet ﷺ and are considered equal to the Qur'an in legislative or creedal weight.

The sound (*ṣaḥiḥ*) hadith and the good (*ḥasan*) hadith number several thousand (the good are a degree slightly lower than the sound, analogous to a B versus an A in grading). According to most scholars, the sound classification is used in legislative but not agreed upon in creedal matters. On the other hand, good hadith are used in legislation and virtuous actions but with more caution than the first two categories. They can also be used to support hadith from the first two in case of obfuscation in a matter.

The third and most extensive category is the weak (*ḍaʿīf*) hadith, and depending upon certain factors analogous to say a D– to C+ in verifiability. However, a hadith considered weak because of some fault in its main chain of transmission can achieve a higher status if its verifiability is strengthened by other chains, leading to an overall high probability of soundness. Moreover, some hadith are considered sound in meaning though weak in chain. Some scholars will use weak hadith even for legal proofs in the absence of more sound traditions: Imām Aḥmad b. Ḥanbal, for example, is well known to have preferred weak transmissions to the opinions of men in legal matters.

Some of the hadith in this collection are categorized as weak (*ḍaʿīf*). However, they should be considered genuine sayings of the Prophet ﷺ, though with less reliability than either good or sound transmissions, for a weak hadith has never been considered forged. (Forged hadith fall into an entirely different category.) The weak hadith have simply been relegated to use only as counsel regarding virtuous deeds and acts of charity. The reason they cannot be used for legislation is that only the highest levels of reliability are accepted for such a grave matter; if there is reasonable probability that a hadith is inaccurate or less than authentic, it is not used for creedal or legal matters. It is, however, traditionally encouraged for matters of devotional practice that do not involve legal rulings, either penal or civil.

## UNNECESSARY DISSENSION OVER "WEAK" HADITH

Unfortunately, many modern Muslims have been indoctrinated into uncritically attacking hadith in this third category simply because they are "weak." This is the result of a movement in the last century that desired to place Islam on a "rational" footing and to remove any traditions that diminished its claims to rationality. A purge of Qur'anic commentaries began, and many of the traditional stories that Muslims had borrowed from the Jews and the Christians were attacked as well. Also, because several early scholars condemned the weak hadith, many modern Muslims dismissed weak hadith as unworthy of consideration.

This is a mistake, based on lack of information and a faulty method of reasoning. We cannot read correctly the scholarly statements that condemn weak hadith without taking into account the overall scholarly debate on the subject. If we discounted weak hadith without considering the traditional consensus of hadith scholars, we would end up rejecting some of the most beautiful statements attributed to the Prophet Muhammad ﷺ and would do so unjustly and in opposition to the majority of hadith experts throughout Islamic history.

Here, for example, is a very brief selection from the learned debate among sound scholars who were experts in hadith.

Sīdī ʿAbdallāh b. Ḥajj Ibrāhīm, who abridged the famous didactic poem the *Alfiyyah* of al-ʿIrāqī, says:

> If the [hadith] is not traced reliably back to the chosen [Prophet], [the opinion about its use is either] complete prohibition or complete permissibility.

Commenting on this verse, Imām Ḥasan Mashat says:

> The opinion that a weak hadith is prohibited is that of Qāḍī Abū Bakr b. al-ʿArabī. He opined that even virtuous deeds and acts of devotion not related to law are nonetheless derived from the sacred law, and to use unreliable hadith is akin to possibly innovating acts of worship that God has not sanctioned. Regarding its permissibility, the opinion of Imām Aḥmad b. Ḥanbal is used, and according to a statement attributed to him, "A weak hadith is preferable to the opinion of men." You should know, however, that the opinion that weak hadith should not be used is contrary to the consensus that Imām Sakhāwī says Imām Nawawī mentioned in several of his writings. The consensus is that weak hadith are to be used in meritorious acts of devotion specifically.[1]

Shaykh Muḥammad Jamāluddīn al-Qāsimī, the Syrian master of hadith sciences, a scholar who inclined strongly toward the opinions of Imām Ibn Taymiyyah, writes:

> There are three opinions given concerning weak hadith: the first is they are not used ... ; the second is that they are used without restraint ... ; and the third is that they are used only for meritorious acts of devotion, and this is the soundest position. Imām Ibn ʿAbdal Barr says, "Hadith relating to meritorious acts do not demand the rigors of other types

---

1 Shaykh Ḥasan Mashat ʿAlī Mandhumat Sīdī ʿAbdullāh Ould Ḥājj Ibrāhīm. *Rafʿu Astār*. 1990. (Mecca.) 65.

> of hadith." Imām al-Ḥākim said, "I heard Abū Zakariyya al-ʿAnbarī say, '[In the case of] any hadith that does not permit something prohibited, or prohibit something permissible, or oblige anyone to an act, and that which relates to meritorious matters of commission or omission, I go easy on [it] and cast a blind eye toward [it], concerning the rigorous reliability of its transmitters.'"[2]

Imām Suyūṭī says in his *Tadrīb*:

> Ibn Ḥajar gives three conditions for the use of weak hadith:
> 1) It is not very unreliable
> 2) It is in accordance with already proven principles
> 3) If one does act upon it, it is done so without believing it is absolutely established.[3]

What should be clear from the above is that there was a difference of opinion in early Islam that led to heated debates, and thus the words of great scholars condemning the use of weak hadith have been faithfully recorded; but more importantly, the majority of scholars did not concur as to the prohibition of using weak hadith. On the contrary, later scholars reached a consensus as to their permissibility.

### SOPHISTRY VERSUS SOUND REASONING

Sophists often use a well known fallacious technique in their unsound reasoning: they present only those views that support their premises. This is done in countless pamphlets today that are distributed free of charge in mosques around the world, misleading Muslims who have neither the time nor the training to fully investigate the matter themselves. Any researcher with an adequate knowledge of Arabic and access to sound texts on the science of hadith could author a pamphlet with sound narrations from some of the greatest scholars of Islam proving "categorically" that weak hadith are an abomination

2 Imām Muḥammad Jamāluddīn al-Qāsimī. *Qawāʿid at-Taḥdīth*. 1987. (Beirut: Dār an-Nafā'is). 117.

3 Ibid. 119.

and should not be used. Conversely, using the very same books to quote scholars of equal stature, the same researcher could produce a pamphlet proving that the use of weak hadith is valid as long as the one doing so adheres to the above-stated conditions of Ibn Ḥajar.

In fact, both positions exist, and scholars of the respective positions argued initially with great passion and unassailable belief that their own position was right. As time passed, however, both positions were examined in the light of all the arguments and those who made them. Later scholars concluded that the soundest position was permissibility, and that position has been taught in the great teaching institutions of Islam for many centuries.

In any argument, the fairest and most faithful method is to present both sides and then, if there is one, present the preponderant position. Educated people are then free to choose which position they feel comfortable with. In the case of debates concerning religious matters, the Prophet's ﷺ advice is useful: "Be with the majority of Muslims," and "Difference in my community is a mercy from God." The Qur'an reminds us that good people are those "who hear words and follow the best from them."

Our scholars gave sound and safe advice in their sanctioning of weak hadith, with the caveat that conditions must be fulfilled. The use of weak hadith for meritorious acts has been the practice of the Muslim community for centuries, and a well-known principle in the axioms of juristic methodology states, "Matters of difference should never be attacked." This applies, of course, when the difference is among rightly guided scholars working within the orthodoxy established by the early first three centuries of Islam, those who have been recognized by the community of scholars over the centuries as being independent scholars unfettered by precedent. Also, the matter must not be something any previous generation of scholars had reached a consensus about.

If disinterested Muslims would adhere to these wonderful

principles, the majority of problems in our community that involve religious dissension would end. Ramadan moon-sighting debates would cease, as would arguments over the *Mawlid*,[4] *Burda*,[5] *inshād*,[6] and recitation of the Qur'an for the dead or in groups. Our rightly guided scholars of the past resolved such matters and countless other debates centuries ago. This reflects the beautiful diversity and freedom of practice within reasonable limits among our scholars. Their differing positions and even harsh and strong words (on both sides) can be used by ignorant people today to confuse, divide, and even lead astray people who don't understand the nuances of juristic reasoning and the possibility of having more than one valid practice or position on any given matter.

I have translated this collection hoping to inspire people to practice good character with each other, overlook faults, desire mercy for others that mercy might be shown them, and to practice that noble prophetic example of treating others as indeed we ourselves would like to be treated.

4 Traditional celebration of the Prophet Muḥammad's ﷺ birthday.

5 Famous poem about the Prophet Muḥammad ﷺ traditionally sung throughout the Muslim world.

6 Devotional songs.

# Biographies of the Narrators

## ABŪ DĀWŪD

Sulaymān b.[7] al-Ashʿab b. Isḥāq b. Bashīr al-Azadī as-Sijistanī, popularly known as Abū Dāwūd, was born in 202 AH[8]/817 CE in Sijistan, Persia (located in present day Iran). During his life, he traveled in search of knowledge of hadith, which took him to Baghdad, the Hijaz (Western Arabia), Egypt, Al-Jazirah, Nishapur, Syria, and Isfahan. His journey in search of prophetic narrations resulted in his studying under many of the prominent hadith scholars of the day, including Imām Aḥmad b. Ḥanbal and Imām al-Bukhārī.

At-Tirmidhī and an-Nisā'ī are among Abū Dāwūd's students. He is known for his compilation of 4,800 hadith in his book entitled *As-Sunan Abū Dāwūd*, about which he commented, "I wrote down 500,000 hadith from the Prophet ﷺ, of which I selected those which are in *As-Sunan*."

Muḥammad b. Isḥāq as-Saghanī said, "Hadith was made subject to Abū Dāwūd as iron was made subject to Prophet Dāwūd ﷺ."

Mūsa b. Ibrāhīm, a great scholar of hadith, once said of him, "Abū Dāwūd was created in this world for hadith and in the next world for Paradise. I have never seen better than he."

Al-Ḥākim said of him, "Abū Dāwūd was the undisputed

7 b.: abbreviation of "*bin*," which means "son of".

8 AH is the abbreviation for "After the Hijrah." The *Hijrah*, which marks the beginning of the Muslim calendar, is the migration of the Prophet Muḥammad ﷺ from Mecca to Medina which took place in 622 CE (Christian Era).

Imām of the people of hadith in his age."

Commenting on Imām Abū Dāwūd's hadith collection, Ibn al-Jawzī said, "Abū Dāwūd was an eminent doctor of hadith and an outstanding scholar. No one has compiled a book like his *Sunan*."

A *ḥāfiẓ* (hadith master)[9], Imām Abū Dāwūd is said to have been able to commit a book to memory by reading it only once. He used to have one of his sleeves widened in order to store notes on hadith in it but felt that widening the other sleeve was excessive. In addition to being a great scholar, Abū Dāwūd was known to lead a pious and austere lifestyle in which he devoted much time to worship and the remembrance of God, the Most High.

The Imām passed away in 275 AH/889 CE in the city of Basra during the lunar month of Shawwāl.[10] May God be pleased with him.

### ABŪ NUʿAYM

Aḥmad b. ʿAbdullāh b. Aḥmad b. Isḥāq b. Mūsa b. Mahran al-Asbahānī is known as Abū Nuʿaym. He was born in 336 AH/948 CE in Isfahan into a scholarly family. At a very young age, he began studying hadith with his father who himself was a hadith scholar. Imām Abū Nuʿaym later went on to study hadith from numerous teachers, including at-Ṭabarānī, Abū ash-Shaykh, al-Ḥākim, and al-Ajūrrī.

Imām Abū Nuʿaym's chains of transmission are known for two unique characteristics: first, he possesses some chains that none of his contemporaries acquired, as he is the only one of them to have received his chains from so many scholars. (The drawback to this, however, is that some of these scholars are otherwise unheard of, so the chains of narration he possesses from these particular scholars are unverifiable.) Secondly, because of his very long life and his early start in learning

---

9 A hadith master (*ḥāfiẓ*) is one who has memorized a minimum of 100,000 hadith.

10 All of the months mentioned are the lunar months of the Islamic Hijrī calendar.

hadith, his chains of narration are unusually short. Since short chains are highly sought after by scholars of hadith, many wished to study with Imām Abū Nuʿaym; his students include al-Khaṭīb, al-Malinī, and his brother Abū ʿAlī al-Ḥasan.

A prolific writer, Imām Abū Nuʿaym authored numerous works including *Faḍilāt al-ʿĀdilīn min al-Wulāt* (The Merits of Rulers Who are Just), *Al-Mahdī* (The Mahdī), *Dhikr Akhbār Asbahān* (Memorial of the Chronicles of Isfahan), *Al-Mustakhraj ʿalā al-Bukhārī* (Narrations Meeting al-Bukhārī's Criterion), *Al-Mustakhraj ʿalā Muslim* (Narrations Meeting Muslim's Criterion), *Musnad al-Imām Abī Ḥanīfa* (Hadith Narrated by Imām Abū Ḥanīfa), and his famous ten-volume work *Ḥilyat al-Awliyā' wa Tabaqāt al-Aṣfiyā'* (The Adornment of the Saints and the Generations of the Pure Ones), a comprehensive encyclopedia of Sufi personalities that, in the words of the author in his introduction, "comprises the names and some of the sayings and words of the eminent true Sufis and their Imāms ... from the generation of the Companions, their Successors, and those who came after them." Imām Abū Nuʿaym is perhaps best known for this work.

Though some people criticize Imām Abū Nuʿaym, claiming there are forged hadith in his *Ḥilyah*, scholars have defended him and approved of his hadith as sound since he always names his narrators, allowing one to assess the reliability of every report he cites. Imām Abū Nuʿaym passed away in Isfahan, his birthplace, in 430 AH/1038 CE. May God be pleased with him.

AD-DAYLAMĪ (the father)

Abū Shujāʿ Shayruya b. Shahardār b. Shayruya ad-Daylamī was born in the year 440 AH/1048 CE. He was a hadith master (*ḥāfiẓ*) and historian. Little is known about his life except that he traveled far and wide, was of excellent physique and manners, was very intelligent, was reserved in speech, and worked as a teaching assistant in a college in Ḥamadān in present day Iran. Among his teachers were Abū al-Faḍl Muḥammad b. ʿUthmān al-Qumaṣānī, Yūsuf b. Muḥammad b. Yūsuf al-

Mustamlī, and Abū Nāṣir az-Zaynabī. His students included his son, Shahardār, Muḥammad b. al-Faḍl al-Isfarayinī, and Abū Mūsa al-Madinī. Adh-Dhahabī relates a hadith in which Imām ad-Daylamī is one of the narrators. The sources that mention Imām Abū Shujāᶜ ad-Daylamī mention only three books authored by him, one of which is *Kitāb al-Firdaws al-Akhbar*. Another of his books is a historical work titled *Tarīkh al-Ḥamadān*.

Imām Abū Shujāᶜ Ad-Daylamī died on the 19th day of the lunar month of Rajab in the year 509 AH/1115 CE. May God have mercy on him.

### AD-DAYLAMĪ (THE SON)

Abū Mansūr Shahardār b. al-Ḥafiẓ Shayruya b. Shahardār ad-Daylamī was born in the year 483 AH/1090 CE. He was a hadith master, imam, scholar, and author. As-Samaᶜanī said that he was also knowledgeable of proper *adab* (manners) and that he was mild mannered and jocular. He often retired to the mosque for worship and study and followed in his father's footsteps, writing hadith, listening to them, and seeking them. He traveled to Isfahan with his father and then to Baghdad, where he listened to and narrated hadith.

Adh-Dhahabī also mentioned that Imām ad-Daylamī studied in Baghdad. Among his teachers were his father, Shayruya b. Shahardār, Abū al-Fatāḥ ᶜAbdus b. ᶜAbdullāh, and Fayd b. ᶜAbd ar-Raḥman ash-Shaᶜarānī. Among his students were his son, Abū Muslim Aḥmad, as well as Abū Saᶜīd as-Samaᶜanī, from whom adh-Dhahabī narrates hadith. His most popular book is *Musnad al-Firdaws*, in which he narrates hadith that his father transmitted to him as well as other hadith. Imām ad-Daylamī passed away in the lunar month of Rajab in the year 558 AH/1163 CE. May God have mercy on him.

### AL-BAYHAQĪ

Aḥmad b. al-Ḥusayn b. ᶜAlī, also known as Abū Bakr al-Bayhaqī, was born in Khasrajand, a village around Bayhaq, which is close to Nishapur, Persia (present-day Iran), in 384 AH/994 CE. Raised in Bayhaq, he traveled in search of sacred knowledge to Baghdad, Kufa, Mecca, and other cities. Among his numerous teachers in jurisprudence was Imām Abū al-Fatḥ Nāsir b. al-Ḥusayn b. Muḥammad al-Qurashī al-ʿUmarī al-Marwazī ash-Shāfiʿī an-Naysāburī. His teachers in hadith include al-Ḥākim an-Naysaburī, as well as al-Ḥākim's teacher, as-Sayyid Abū'l-Ḥasan Muḥammad b. al-Ḥusayn b. Dāwūd al-ʿAlawī al-Ḥasanī an-Naysaburī al-Ḥasib.

Imām adh-Dhahabī said of him, "Had Bayhaqī wanted to found his own school of jurisprudence and be its *mujtahid* [highest ranking scholar who determines rulings], he would have been able to do so because of the vast range of subjects of which he was a master and because of his knowledge of scholarly differences."

Imām al-Ḥaramayn al-Juwaynī once said, "Every Shāfiʿī scholar is indebted to Shāfiʿī except for Bayhaqī, to whom Shāfiʿī is indebted. This is because Bayhaqī wrote several works which strengthened Imām Shāfiʿī's school, expanded questions upon which the Imām had been brief, and supported his positions."

Imām al-Bayhaqī led a pious and ascetic lifestyle; for the last 30 years of his life, he fasted most days except those in which it is forbidden to fast. He authored nearly a thousand volumes, writing on the sciences of hadith, Quranic exegesis (*tafsīr*), sacred law, and other subjects. Among his books are *Al-Asmā' wa's-Sifāt* (The Divine Names and Attributes), *Al-Iʿtiqād ʿalā Madhhab as-Salaf Ahl as-Sunna wa'l-Jamāʿa* (Islamic Doctrines According to the School of the Pious Predecessors), and *Dalā'il an-Nubuwwa* (The Signs of Prophethood). He died in Nishapur on 458 AH/1065 CE. May God bless him and fill his grave with light.

AL-BAZZĀR

Aḥmad b. ʿAmr b. ʿAbd al-Khāliq Abū Bakr al-Bazzār was of Basran lineage. He attained the rank of hadith master and was among the foremost of scholars of hadith. He authored several books on hadith, including *musnads* (collections of hadith arranged hierarchically according to the first authority in the chain of narration). One is titled *Al-Baḥr az-Zākhir* (The Abounding Ocean) and is also known as *Al-Musnad al-Kabīr* (The Grand Musnad). He also authored smaller collections of hadith.

Imām al-Bazzār had several teachers including aṭ-Ṭabarānī. Towards the end of his life, he narrated hadith in Isfahan, Baghdad, and Syria. Imām al-Bazzār died in Ramlah in 292 AH/905 CE. May God fill his grave with light.

### AL-BUKHĀRĪ

Muḥammad b. Ismāʿīl b. Ibrāhīm b. al-Mughīrah al-Bukhārī al-Jiʿfī is known as Imām al-Bukhārī and is often also referred to as Abū ʿAbdullāh. He was born on a Friday in the lunar month of Shawwāl in the year 194 AH/810 CE in Bukhāra, which is in modern-day Uzbekistan, where he grew up as an orphan. He began his Islamic education in the *kuttāb* (traditional Qur'an school), where he quickly took an interest in studying hadith. As he himself later recollected, he memorized several books of hadith by the age of sixteen before setting off with his mother and brother, Aḥmad, for Mecca in the pursuit of knowledge. His passion for collecting prophetic narrations took him to the farthest corners of the Islamic world, allowing him to narrate from thousands of teachers, including Imām Aḥmad b. Ḥanbal (d. 241 AH/855 CE), Yaḥya b. Maʿin (d. 233 AH/848 CE), and Isḥāq b. Rahawayh (d. 238 AH/852 CE). His inspiration to author a collection of hadith that would include only rigorously authentic narrations stemmed from his teacher, Isḥāq b. Rahawayh, who often said to his students, "I wish that you would produce a concise book, including in it only the rigorously authenticated narrations of the Messenger of God ﷺ." The monumental task of compiling approximately 4400 rigorously authenticated narrations out of the total 600,000 narrations he had collected took Imām al-Bukhārī sixteen years.

Students who narrate hadith from Imām al-Bukhārī include such luminaries in the field as Imām Muslim (d. 261 AH/875 CE), at-Tirmidhī (d. 279 AH/892 CE), an-Nasā'ī (d. 303 AH/915 CE), and Ibn Abī ad-Dunya (d. 281 AH/894 CE), not to mention countless others who are not as widely known. Imām al-Bukhārī authored many books; among them are *Al-Jāmiᶜ aṣ-Ṣaḥiḥ* (The Rigorously Authenticated Collection), *Al-Asmā' wa'l-Kuna* (Names and Agnomens), *At-Tarīkh al-Kabīr* (The Grand Historical Account), *Qaḍāya aṣ-Ṣaḥāba wa't-Tābiᶜīn* (Legal Judgments of the Companions and the Followers), *Khalqu Afᶜāl al-ᶜIbād* (The Creation of Human Action), and *Al-Adab al-Mufrad* (Etiquettes and Manners).

Anecdotes demonstrating both his legendary photographic memory and his profound, sincere devotion to God and His Messenger ﷺ abound. While still a student, many of his contemporaries would trust his memory over their own handwritten notes from the same class. The widespread acceptance by Muslims over the ages of his *Ṣaḥiḥ* is commonly interpreted as a result of his sincerity in compiling it. Near the end of his life, he retreated to a small town named Khartank (in modern-day Azerbaijan); after witnessing the moral afflictions from which the Prophet ﷺ sought refuge in God, Imām al-Bukhārī lost any desire to remain in this world. He passed away on a Thursday night, the night of ᶜ*Īd al-Fiṭr* in the year 256 AH/870 CE.

### AL-ḤĀKIM

Muḥammad b. ᶜAbdullāh b. Ḥamdawayh b. Naᶜīm ad-Dabī, also known as Abū ᶜAbdullāh al-Ḥākim an-Naysaburī, was born in Nishapur, Persia (in present-day Iran) in the year 321 AH/933 CE. He traveled to Iraq, in the year 341 AH/952 CE, in search of knowledge of prophetic traditions. He also traveled to the Ḥijāz, among other lands, acquiring hadith transmissions from about 2,000 hadith scholars. Among his teachers was Imām Dāraqutnī, who also narrated hadith from him.

Imām al-Ḥākim was appointed as a judge in 359 AH/969

CE; due to this, he was given the nickname "al-Ḥākim" (the Magistrate). He was among the most knowledgeable of scholars with regard to distinguishing authentic hadith from inauthentic ones. It was said that he had no peer in hadith knowledge in Khurasan, the Ḥijāz, Syria, Iraq, Rayy, Tabaristan, and Transoxiana.

Imām al-Ḥākim quickly became famous during his own lifetime. He wrote books on hadith and various other subjects, authoring approximately 1,500 volumes, according to Ibn ʿAsākir. Imām al-Ḥākim wrote histories of scholars as well as books on hadith methodology; he is best known for his four volume *Ḥadīth al-Mustadrik ʿalā aṣ-Ṣaḥīḥayn* (The Addendum to the Two Ṣaḥīḥ Collections of Bukhārī and Muslim), in which he narrates many hadith according to the methods of Bukhārī and Muslim and several according to his own methods. He had a keen memory and lived a pious life. Imām al-Ḥākim died in Nishapur, the town of his birth, in 405 AH/1014 CE. May God have mercy on him.

### AL-KHAṬĪB AL-BAGHDĀDĪ

Aḥmad b. ʿAlī b. Thābit, also known as Abū Bakr al-Khaṭīb al-Baghdādī, was born in Ghuzayya, midway between Kufa and Mecca, in the year 392 AH/1002 CE. He was one of the foremost historians of his generation as well as a hadith master. Raised in Baghdad, his studies began when he was eleven years of age. He then traveled in search of knowledge of hadith to Mecca, Basra, Ad-Dinawar, Kufa, and other cities. He returned to Baghdad after his travels and won the favor of the caliph's vizier. Then, after an attempted coup against the vizier, he fled to Damascus; he later went to some other cities before finally returning to Damascus. He heard hadith from many scholars including the famous female master Karīma b. Aḥmad b. Muḥammad al-Marwaziyya. He received a license from her to teach *Ṣaḥīḥ Bukhārī* within a span of five days while on Hajj.

Among the special qualities related about Imām al-Khaṭīb

are that he spoke pure classical Arabic and had accurate and elegant handwriting. It is reported that he recited the Qur'an in its entirety each morning and evening while on a journey from Damascus to Baghdad. His most famous work is his 14-volume *Tarīkh Baghdād* (History of Baghdad). Among his other works is *Al-Jāmiʿ li Akhlāq ar-Rawī wa Adāb as-Sāmiʿ*, a book that describes the proper ethics and manners that should be possessed by hadith narrators and auditors.

Imām al-Khaṭīb had many students; among them were two Ḥanbalīs, Abū Ya'la and master of hadith Ibn ʿAqīl. Ibn Ḥajar said about Imām al-Khaṭīb, "There is hardly a single discipline among the sciences of hadith in which al-Khaṭīb did not author a monograph."

Imām adh-Dhahabī called Imām al-Khaṭīb, "the most peerless imam, erudite scholar and *mufti*, meticulous hadith master, foremost scholar of his time in hadith, prolific author, and seal of the hadith masters."

Imām Ibn Nuqta said of him, "Whoever gives credit where credit is due knows that hadith scholars, after al-Khaṭīb, all depend on his books."

Imām Saʿīd al-Mu'addib asked al-Khaṭīb, "Are you the hadith master, Abū Bakr?" He replied, "I am Aḥmad b. ʿAlī. Hadith mastership ended with ad-Dāraqutnī."

Imām Abū Isḥāq al-Isfarayinī said, "Al-Khaṭīb is the Dāraqutnī of our time."

In his final illness before his death, Imām al-Khaṭīb donated his money and property to charitable causes as well as to the scholars. He died in Baghdad in 463 AH/1070 CE. May God have mercy on him.

### AR-RĀFIʿĪ

ʿAbd al-Karīm b. Muḥammad b. ʿAbd al-Karīm b. al-Faḍl b. al-Ḥasan, also known as Abū al-Qāsim ar-Rāfiʿī, was born in 557 AH/1162 CE in the town of Qazvin, Persia (in modern-day Iran). He and Imām Nawawī are the two principal scholars of the late Shāfiʿī school, as they researched and established the main opinions of the school. Imām ar-Rāfiʿī was a great scholar of Islamic law as well as Qur'anic exegesis (*tafsīr*). Imām Tāj ad-Dīn Subkī said about him, "Imām ar-Rāfiʿī was filled with knowledge of the sciences of sacred law, Qur'anic exegesis, hadith, and fundamentals of Islamic legal methodology, towering above his contemporaries in the transmission of evidence, in research, in guidance, and in attainment of spiritual rank. It was as if jurisprudence had been dead, and he revived it and spread it, raising its foundations after ignorance had killed and buried it."

Imām ar-Rāfiʿī wrote books on sacred law and history, of which his main work was a commentary on Imām al-Ghazālī's *Al-Wajīz*, titled *Fatḥ al-ʿAzīz fī sh-Sharḥ al-Wajīz* (The Victory of the Invincible: An Exegesis of "The Synopsis"). Imām Nawawī used this book as a source for his book titled *Minhāj aṭ-Ṭalibīn* (The Seekers' Road).

In addition, Imām ar-Rāfiʿī was a teacher of Qur'anic exegesis and hadith in Qazvin. Among his students was the hadith master Imām Mundhirī.

Imām ar-Rāfiʿī was also known as a pure-hearted ascetic and mystic. Imām Nawawī said of him, "[He] had a firm standing in righteousness, and many miracles were vouchsafed to him."

Imām ar-Rāfiʿī died in his home town of Qazvin in the year 623 AH/1226 CE. May God have mercy on him.

### AL-ṬABARĀNĪ

Sulaymān b. Aḥmad b. Ayyūb b. Muṭayr al-Lakhamī ash-Shāmī, also known as Abū'l-Qāsim aṭ-Ṭabarānī, is considered one of the greatest scholars of hadith. He was born in 260 AH/873 CE in Acre, Palestine. His lineage traces back to Tabariya, Sham (present day Palestine, Jordan, and Syria), and because of this, he is referred to as aṭ-Ṭabarānī. He traveled for sixteen years to the Hijaz, Yemen, Egypt, Iraq, Persia, and the Arabian Peninsula in order to learn from the masters of hadith. During this time, he met with approximately one thousand scholars. He eventually settled in Isfahan, Persia, where he taught hadith for sixty years and wrote many useful books. In addition to authoring books of Qur'anic exegesis (*tafsīr*) and proofs of prophecy (*dalā'il an-nubuwa*), he compiled three lexicons of hadith in which he listed the names of the scholars of hadith alphabetically. These three lexicons are titled, *Al-Muᶜjam al-Kabīr*, *Al-Muᶜjam al-Awsaṭ*, and *Al-Muᶜjam aṣ-Ṣaghīr*, the largest of which consists of twenty-five volumes. He once said that the secret to his acquisition of so many hadith was to sleep on reed mats for thirty years. Aṭ-Ṭabarānī died in Isfahan, a hundred years after his birth, in the year 360 AH/970 CE. May God bless him.

### AT-TIRMIDHĪ

Muḥammad b. ᶜĪsā b. Sūrah b. Mūsā, also known as Abū ᶜĪsā as-Sulamī at-Tirmidhī, was born in 209 AH/824 CE in Termez, which is in present-day Uzbekistan. He traveled to Khurasan, Medina, and Mecca in search of knowledge and became a hadith master and an imam. He was a student of al-Bukhārī, Isḥāq b. Rahawayh, and others, and he compiled a book of hadith called *Al-Jāmiᶜ al-Kabīr*, which is also known as *Ṣaḥīḥ at-Tirmidhī*. It is considered one of the "Six Ṣaḥīḥ" collections of hadith: Bukhārī, Muslim, Abū Dāwūd, Nasā'ī, at-Tirmidhī, and Ibn Mājah (this order is the most popular ranking of these collections). Additionally, Imām at-Tirmidhī wrote on other topics, including history and the prophetic traits. His book *Ash-Shamā'il an-Nabawiyya* (The Characteristics of the Prophet) provides a detailed description of the Prophet ﷺ. Imām at-Tirmidhī also composed a book on hadith methodology called *Al-ᶜIlal* (The Discrepancies).

Several scholars reported that Imām at-Tirmidhī had a prodigious memory; he was able to retain numerous hadith after hearing them only once. Students came from all over to study with Imām at-Tirmidhī, the most famous of whom were Haysam b. Kulayb and Abū'l-ᶜAbbās. Though he lost his sight towards the end of his life, Imām at-Tirmidhi's keen memory continued to remind him of his surroundings; it is reported that in spite of his blindness, he once lowered his head on a journey at the moment when he expected to pass under a low tree limb. ʿUmar b. ʿAlaq once said, "Bukhārī died without leaving anyone in Khurasan who compared with Abū ʿIsā (at-Tirmidhī) in knowledge, memory, piety, and abstinence." After contributing tremendously to the teaching and preservation of Islam, Imām at-Tirmidhī died in Termez in the year 279 AH/892 CE. May God fill his grave with light.

## IBN ʿABD AL-BARR

Yūsuf b. ʿAbdullāh b. Muḥammad b. ʿAbd al-Barr was born in Andalusia (Muslim Spain), in the city of Cordoba, in the year 368 AH/ 978 CE. He was a *ḥāfiẓ* (hadith master), historian, genealogist, author, and Mālikī scholar. He was nicknamed "The Hadith Master of the West." He went on long journeys throughout Andalusia in search of hadith. He was appointed as a judge on several occasions and was highly respected by his scholarly peers for his knowledge of hadith. Imām al-Qurṭubī cites him roughly five hundred times in his famous book of Qur'anic exegesis. The Ẓahirī scholar Imām Ibn Ḥazm complimented Imām Ibn ʿAbd al-Barr's book, *At-Tamhīd*, saying, "I do not know of anything like it, let alone better than it, with regard to the superlative understanding of hadith."

Imām Ibn ʿAbd al-Barr was the foremost scholar in his time in both memory and precision. He authored books on a variety of subjects including hadith, sacred law, biographies of famous Muslims, canonical Qur'anic readings (*qira'āt*), genealogy, and history. One of the most famous of his books is the two-volume biographical work *Al-Istīʿāb fī Asmā' al-Aṣḥāb* (The Comprehensive Compilation of the Names of the Prophet's Companions). He died in Shatiba in 463 AH/1070 CE. May God have mercy on him.

### IBN ABĪ AD-DUNYĀ

ᶜAbdullāh b. Muḥammad b. ᶜUbayd b. Sufyan b. Qays al-Qurashī is known as Ibn Abī ad-Dunyā. He was born in the year 208 AH/823 CE. He traveled little, and this affected the number of versions he was able to collect for any one particular hadith. He narrates from a large number of scholars, many of whom are not well known. The oldest of his teachers is Saᶜīd b. Sulayman b. Saᶜdawayh al-Wasiṭī, and the best known is Imām al-Bukhārī. Those who narrate from him include al-Hārith b. Abī Usāmah (from whom he also narrates), Ibn Abī Ḥātim, and Ibn Mājah in his book on Qur'anic exegesis (*tafsīr*).

Imām Ibn Abī ad-Dunyā was a prolific author; his books contain treasures of hadith not found in other collections. Among his books are *Kitāb al-Mawt wa'l-Qubūr* (The Book of Death and Graves), *Kitāb al-Manām* (The Book of Dreams), *Dhamm al-Malāhī* (Criticism of Things Which Distract), *Al-Faraj* (The Deliverance), and *Kitāb al-Ikhwān* (The Book of Brothers). Many consider him a reliable hadith transmitter, though, like many hadith scholars, he does not restrict himself to only rigorously authenticated narrations in his books.

Imām al-Khaṭīb al-Baghdādī mentions that Imām Ibn Abī ad-Dunyā was a private tutor to many of the children of the ᶜAbbāsid caliph. He died in 281 AH/894 CE. May God have mercy on him and fill his grave with light.

### IBN AL-MUBĀRAK

ᶜAbdullāh b. al-Mubārak b. Wadih, also known as Abū ᶜAbd ar-Rahmān al-Hanzalī at-Tamīmī, was born in Merv, a village near Khurasan, in present-day Turkmenistan, in 118 AH/736 CE. He was given the title "Shaykh al-Islām" and was a hadith master, merchant, author, and traveler. He also fought in battles in defense of Islam and Muslims.

Ibn al-Mubārak spent most of his life traveling, whether for Ḥajj, jihād, or trade. He mastered knowledge of hadith, jurisprudence (*fiqh*), and Arabic. He was also known for his bravery and generosity. He sat in circles of knowledge composed of many great scholars of his time, including Imām Mālik and ath-Thawrī, and he studied with al-Layth and many others. Ibn Mahdī, ʿAbdu'r-Razzāq, Yaḥyā b. al-Qattān, Ibn Wahb, and others relate from him.

Imām Ibn Ḥanbal said, "During the time of Ibn al-Mubārak, there was no one who sought after knowledge more than he. He traveled to Yemen, Egypt, Syria, the Hijaz, Basra, and Kufa in search of sacred knowledge."

Imām Ibn Waḍḍāh said, "Ibn al-Mubārak related about 25,000 hadith. He was once asked, 'Up until when did you study knowledge?' To this, Ibn al-Mubārak responded, 'I hope that you will find me doing that until I die!'"

Describing knowledge, Imām Ibn al-Mubārak used to say, "Knowledge begins with the intention [to seek it]; then follows listening, then understanding, then action, then preservation, and then spreading it." He also said, "The trace of ink on the garment of the master of hadith is better than perfume on a bride's garment."

Imām Ibn al-Mubārak died by the Euphrates in Hīt, Iraq, upon leaving a battle with the Byzantines, in 181 AH/797 CE. May God bless him and fill his grave with light.

### IBN AN-NAJJĀR

Muḥammad b. Aḥmad b. ʿAbd al-ʿAzīz, also known as Abū'l-Baqā' al-Futūḥī al-Ḥanbalī (an-Najjār), was born in 898 AH/1492 CE. He was given the title, "Shaykh al-Islām" and was an Egyptian Ḥanbalī scholar, judge, and author. ʿAbd al-Wahhāb Shaʿrānī once said of him, "I kept his company for 40 years and never saw him commit a reprehensible act, nor did I see anyone who spoke better than he or showed more politeness to those he sat with."

Imām an-Najjār died in 972 AH/1564 CE. May God have mercy on him and fill his grave with light.

### IBN ʿASĀKIR

ʿAlī b. Abī Muḥammad al-Ḥasan b. Hibatullāh b. ʿAbdullāh b. al-Ḥusayn is known as Ibn ʿAsākir and nicknamed Abū'l-Qāsim. He was born into a scholarly family in the beginning of the lunar month of Muḥarram in the year 499 AH/1105 CE. His brother began narrating hadith to him when he was only six years old. At the age of twenty-one, Imām Ibn ʿAsākir set off in pursuit of knowledge, traveling first to Iraq, then to Mecca, and then to Khurasan through Azerbaijan. He acquired knowledge from approximately 1,300 teachers, including luminaries such as al-Qāḍī Abū Bakr, and he acquired teaching licenses (*ijāzāt*) from 290 scholars. Interestingly, the list of his teachers includes the names of about eighty scholarly women.

Imām Ibn ʿAsākir is known to have taught and narrated hadith in Baghdad, al-Hijaz, Isfahan, and Nishapur. In 533 AH/1138 CE, he returned to Damascus and taught hadith in the Umayyad Mosque. He later taught at the *Dār al-Ḥadīth* school, built for him by Sultan Nūr ad-Dīn b. Zankī, who was the uncle of Ṣalāḥ ad-Dīn (Saladin) al-Ayyubī. Many scholars narrate hadith from him, most notably al-Ḥafiẓ Abū'l-ʿAlā' al-ʿAṭṭār, al-Ḥafiẓ Abū Saʿd as-Samʿānī, and his son, al-Qāsim b. ʿAlī.

Whereas in earlier times there were often tens of erudite hadith masters in a single generation, Imām Ibn ʿAsākir was unmatched in his generation, "collecting that which others had not," as as-Samʿānī says, "and towering above his contemporaries." He is widely respected for the breadth and depth of his knowledge in hadith and the accuracy of his narration. A prolific writer, Imām Ibn ʿAsākir authored many books, including the seven-volume *As-Subaʿiyyat* (The Sevens), which lists narrations with chains containing only seven narrators up to the Prophet ﷺ. He also wrote *Al-Musalsalāt* (The Chained Narrations), which contains hadith with uniqueness in their chains, and he authored *Arbaʿūn Ḥadīthan ʿan Arbaʿīna Shaykhan min Arbaʿīna Madina* (Forty Hadith Narrated from Forty Shaykhs from Forty Cities). His eighty-volume *Tarīkh Dimashq* (The History of Damascus) is itself enough for a lifetime's work.

Imām Ibn ʿAsākir passed away in the month of Rajab in the year 571 AH/1176 CE. Al-Quṭb an-Naysāburī led his funeral prayer, which Sulṭān Ṣalāḥ ad-Dīn (Saladin) personally attended. Imām Ibn ʿAsākir is buried in Damascus in the Bāb aṣ-Ṣaghīr cemetery, next to his father, near the grave of Caliph Muʿāwiya b. Abī Sufyan. May God bless him.

### IBN ḤIBBĀN

Muḥammad b. Ḥibbān b. Aḥmad b. Ḥibbān b. Muʿādh b. Maʿbad, also known as Abū Ḥātim at-Tamimī al-Bustī, was born in Bust, Sijistan, located in present-day Afghanistan. It is said that he was a historian, a scholar of Islam (*ʿālim*), a geographer, and a scholar of hadith (*muḥaddith*). He traveled in search of knowledge of hadith to Khurasan, Sham, Egypt, Iraq, the Arabian Peninsula, and Nishapur. He later returned to his native city of Bust and then served as a judge in Samarqand for a period of time. He was one of the most prolific writers; about him Yaqūt once said, "He produced works in the sciences of hadith that no one else could have written." Among his books is *Al-Musnad aṣ-Ṣaḥīḥ*, a collection of hadith about which it is said, "It is sounder than the *Sunan* of Ibn Mājah." It is also known by the title *Al-Anwāʿ wa't-Taqāsīm* (Types and Categories). He wrote other works in hadith, encyclopedism, biography, and history. Ibn Ḥibbān died in the town in which he was born, Bust, in the year 354 AH/965 CE. May God grant him mercy.

### IBN MĀJAH

Muḥammad b. Yazīd ar-Rub'i, also known as Abū ʿAbdullāh b. Mājah al-Qazwinī, was born in Qazvin, Persia (present-day Iran), in the year 209 AH/824 CE. He was a *ḥāfiẓ* (hadith master), Imām, and Qur'anic exegete (*mufassir*). He traveled in search of sacred knowledge to Basra, Baghdad, Syria, Cairo, the Hijaz, and Rayy. He studied under many great scholars.

Imām Ibn Mājah had many students of his own as well. His collection of hadith, called the *Sunan* (Prophetic Examples), is counted among the "Six Ṣaḥīḥ" collections of hadith: Bukhārī, Muslim, Abū Dāwūd, Nasā'ī, Tirmidhī, and Ibn Mājah.

The Imām passed away in 273 AH/886 CE. May God have mercy on him.

IMAM AḤMAD B. ḤANBAL

Aḥmad b. Muḥammad b. Ḥanbal b. Hilāl b. Asad is popularly known as Aḥmad b. Ḥanbal and is often also referred to as Abū ᶜAbdillāh. He was born in the lunar month of Rabīᶜ al-Awwal in the year 164 AH/780 CE in Baghdad, where he grew up and spent much of his life. At the age of fifteen, in the same year that Imām Mālik passed away, Imām Aḥmad began the pursuit of sacred knowledge, which took him to the far reaches of the Islamic world. Among his teachers were Abū Yūsuf (d. 182 AH/798 CE), Hushaym b. Bishr al-Wasiṭī (d. 183 AH/799 CE), ᶜAbd ar-Raḥmān b. Mahdī al-Baṣrī (d. 198 AH/813 CE), and Wakīᶜ b. al-Jarraḥ al-Kūfī (d. 197 AH/812 CE). He is known to have met Imām ash-Shāfiᶜī in 195 AH/810 CE, and each of them benefited from the other for the brief time they remained in contact.

After twenty-five years of studying, Imām Aḥmad finally began to teach in Baghdad at the age of forty, narrating hadith and issuing fatwas (legal opinions). Although a founder of one of the four living schools of jurisprudence (*fiqh*) in Islam,[11] he preferred that his legal opinions not be written down out of respect and deference to the hadith, which he saw as far more beneficial and important than the words of scholars. Ibn Jawzī suggests that had he not held this view, it is likely that Imām Aḥmad would have been a prolific writer. While many books are ascribed to him, it is thought that they are mostly collections of his sayings and opinions written down by his students. However, he did author the well-known *Musnad*, in which he collected 30,000 out of 750,000 hadith, many of which are jewels not found in other collections. Abū Zurᶜah

11 Ḥanbalī: one of the four schools of thought traditionally accepted by consensus of the Sunni scholars.

ar-Rāzī said of him, "Aḥmad b. Ḥanbal committed one million hadith to memory." When asked how he knows this, Ar-Rāzī responded, "I studied with him all of the chapters [of hadith]."

Widely respected and loved for both his abstinence and his steadfastness, Imām Aḥmad is perhaps best known for his courage in the face of the persecution he experienced for refusing to support the Muʿtazilite doctrine that the noble Qur'an was created. As a result, he was imprisoned by the Abbasid caliph, al-Ma'mūn, and by his successor, al-Muʿtaṣim. By the time he was finally released, Imām Aḥmad had spent twenty-eight months in prison. The effect of the torture he underwent during this time is said to have left thirty-four scars on his body.

Imām Aḥmad spent his life in abstinent poverty, supporting his family through his own labor, refusing the gifts of the caliphs and the wealthy. He passed away after a brief sickness on the 12th day of the lunar month Rabīʿ al-Awwal in 241 AH/855 CE, at the age of seventy-seven. According to some reports, more than one million people attended his funeral prayer. He is buried in Baghdad, in the graveyard of al-Ḥarbiyyah. May God bless him.

### MUSLIM

Muslim b. al-Ḥajjāj b. Muslim Abū'l-Ḥusayn al-Qushayrī an-Naysabūrī was born in 204 AH/819 CE in Nishapur, a city in present-day Iran. Imām Muslim began his studies at an early age and traveled in search of knowledge to the Hijaz, Egypt, Syria, and Iraq, where he learned hadith from over 220 major scholars of the age. The esteemed teachers with whom he studied during his travels include Imām Aḥmad and Isḥāq b. Rahawayh. His mentor, however, was Imām al-Bukhārī, the author of the hadith collection *Ṣaḥīḥ Bukhārī*, which most scholars deem to be the best and most accurate book of hadith transmitted from the Prophet Muḥammad ﷺ. Although some scholars prefer Imām Muslim's *Ṣaḥīḥ* over Bukhārī's collection due to the high quality of its editorial layout and its concentration on hadith transmission, it is most often ranked second after Bukhārī's.

Moroccan scholars traditionally preferred his *Ṣaḥīḥ* text over all others, and the Malīkī school's scholars wrote several commentaries on it. He was a deeply revered and pious scholar and after al-Bukhārī is the most quoted of hadith masters. May God bless him and sanctify his secret.